Field Guide to

urban gardening

How to Grow Plants, No Matter Where You Live

Kevin Espiritu
of Epic Gardening

COOL
SPRINGS
PRESS

First Published in 2019 by Cool Springs Press, an imprint of The Quarto Group,
100 Cummings Center, Suite 265-D, Beverly, MA 01915, USA.
T (978) 282-9590 F (978) 283-2742 QuartoKnows.com

Cool Springs Press titles are also available at discount for retail, wholesale, promotional, and bulk purchase. For details, contact the Special Sales Manager by email at specialsales@quarto.com or by mail at The Quarto Group, Attn: Special Sales Manager, 100 Cummings Center, Suite 265-D, Beverly, MA 01915, USA.

23 22 21 20   5

ISBN: 978-0-7603-6396-6

Digital edition published in 2019
eISBN: 978-0-7603-6397-3

Library of Congress Cataloging-in-Publication Data available.

Design: Samantha J. Bednarek
Cover Image: Jeannie Phan
Photography: All photos via Shutterstock, except those credited in the captions and Angelica LaVallee (pages 15 [top], 27 [bottom], 38–39, 42–43, 51–52, 74–81, 92 [top], 98–100, 102–103, 113–117, 123, 125, 127–129, 157–158, 178–181, 185–187, 190–191), Birdies Garden Products (pages 6 [middle], 87 [bottom]), Kevin Espiritu (pages 9, 173–175, 221)
Illustration, pages 200 and 201: Seb Westcott, www.iamseb.com

Printed in China

To all budding green thumbs out there:
May this book help you on your growing journey.

Contents

Introduction

Why Urban Gardening?

I could give a market bag full of grandiose reasons why urban gardening is a wonderful pastime to explore: fresher food, less environmental impact, a more beautiful home. But for me, the real reason is simple . . . it's *fun*.

We live in an increasingly digital and disconnected world. Many of us, myself included, are either behind a computer or a steering wheel for much of the day. There's not much time left to explore Mother Nature.

The solution? Bring Mother Nature into your home and start growing plants. Not only is it a wonderful way to reconnect with the natural world, but urban gardening (or suburban, exurban, or any other kind of gardening for that matter) can also fundamentally change your life. You'll get these great benefits:

- fresher, healthier produce that you can eat minutes after harvesting
- a deeper appreciation for the food on your plate
- stronger relationships with your neighbors, friends, and family

My Story

I was a big nerd as a kid. And when I say "big," I mean it. I was always pushing the 100th percentile when it came to height and weight. On top of that, I sported a large poufy head of hair and adult-size glasses to match. I wasn't the coolest kid in school. I gravitated toward activities that I could do on my own. I collected coins and rocks, grew crystals, captured bugs, and played a lot of video games. There's more, but I'll spare you the nerdy details.

One thing I *didn't* do as a child was grow plants. I don't know why, but gardening never hooked me as a kid. It wasn't until after I graduated from college and settled into my first adult apartment that I even considered gardening. It was my first summer post-graduation. After a whirlwind trip through New Zealand and Australia, a new appreciation for nature sparked within me. That summer, my younger brother came home from college for a few months. Usually, he'd hole up in his room and play video games. So I suggested a few alternative things we could do together. I gave him an awesome list of options such as surfing, rock climbing, skateboarding, and . . . gardening.

To my surprise, he picked gardening.

We didn't have much space to grow anything, so we started out by growing basil in containers and cucumbers in a hydroponic system. My brother was in charge of the basil, and I was in charge of the cucumbers. He had the easier job. His basil grew into gigantic, productive plants that were the source of delicious pesto for many months to come. My cucumbers, on the other hand, were bitter, misshapen, and clearly had some nutrient deficiencies. But where my cucumbers failed, the growing experiment succeeded. I had become hooked on growing plants.

I wanted to learn more, so I picked up a job helping Mel Bartholomew. You might recognize his name as the author of *All New Square Foot Gardening*. While working with Mel and his nonprofit foundation, I soaked up as much of his gardening wisdom as I could. It was an invaluable experience and I'll forever be grateful to Mel for giving me an opportunity to work with him.

In 2015, I started Epic Gardening, a website where I share my journey growing plants. As the years went on, Epic Gardening grew to include an Instagram community, a YouTube channel, and a podcast. It began to take on a life of its own, reaching millions of people around the world in many different countries.

Which brings us to today. *Field Guide to Urban Gardening* is the culmination of my experiments growing food in small spaces. Over the years I've grown all manner of plants in small apartments, community garden lots, backyards, front yards, balconies, rooftops, and even closets. I've experimented with more methods and varieties than I can even recall, and they are all fantastic.

Checking all of the boxes in the "super nerd" category.

What I hope to accomplish with this book is to describe to you what I have learned and help you decide which methods make sense for you and your situation. That's why this book is called a "field guide." It won't help you identify birds or trees. It is simply a catalog of the many options that offer people like us the chance to have an amazing gardening experience in any environment. I hope that by the time you have taken it all in you will be able to identify the path that works best for you, and that it helps you create your own special relationship with gardening in general, and urban gardening in particular. I am an urban gardener and it has changed my life. I truly hope that soon you will be able to say the same.

Keep Growing,
Kevin

About This Book

The goal of this book is simple: *to help demystify the secrets of the "green thumb" and show you how to get started in urban gardening, no matter what type of living situation you're in.*

This book covers the following:

Green Thumb Basics

There's an unlimited amount of information about how to grow specific fruits and veggies. What I've done throughout is try to reduce that information into essential knowledge you need to grow a beautiful, productive urban garden.

Urban Growing Methods

The meat of this book consists of in-depth breakdowns of the most practical growing methods for urban spaces, complete with step-by-step projects to get you started growing. These include:

Container Gardening – What I call the "Lego blocks" method. Growing in containers unlocks any living space as a potential growing space, no matter how large or small.

Raised Bed Gardening – The "tried-and-true" method. Raised beds are suitable for most urban environments, as you can make wonderful use of tight spaces to create gardens that are aesthetically pleasing, yet incredibly productive. Learn about raised bed materials, soil mixes, high-density planting, and more.

Vertical Gardening – Vertical gardening is less of a stand-alone method and more of a technique to squeeze even more plants into even smaller amounts of space. Learn all about how plants naturally climb, types of trellises, and DIY vertical garden projects.

Indoor Edibles – The "kitchen garden" method. You might think indoor gardening is limited to houseplants, but with a little creativity, you can grow so much produce, even in a small apartment. Learn about using windowsills effectively, indoor herb gardens, and growing microgreens.

Balconies and Rooftops – Learn how best to use limited space, how to protect crops from wind and heat, and layering techniques to beautify your home.

Hydroponics – The "high-tech" method. Hydroponics sounds intimidating, but once you get started you might find yourself addicted. It's a soilless growing method, meaning you can set up a hydroponic garden *anywhere* you have a little space. Learn the fundamentals of hydroponic gardening and the five different types of hydroponic systems you can build.

Growing Problems

Did you know that around 40 percent of new gardeners never garden the second year? The final chapter is my attempt to make sure you're not in that 40 percent. Gardening is pretty simple, but there are so many things that can go wrong in the garden, and only one bad thing needs to happen to ruin your efforts. Pests, diseases, environmental conditions, and simple gardening mistakes can all lead to poor results. In this section, you'll learn about the most common problems you'll run into when in the urban garden, such as:

- pests
- diseases
- human error
- nutrient deficiencies

One final note before we get into it. For extended resources, and as a huge "thank you" for buying this book, please check out www.epicgardening.com/fieldguide. There, you'll find articles, videos, and audio that expand on the plans and techniques in this book. Think of it as the digital field guide to accompany you along your growing journey.

Urban Garden Gallery

Before we dive in, know that there are many ways you can achieve your urban gardening goals. Take a look at my website, Epic Gardening, for many reader examples that showcase some of the practical growing methods I talk about in this book.

From intricate brick raised beds to gorgeous balconies to simple kitchen herb window planters, growing in small spaces takes many forms. My goal is to show you how to make sense of your growing options, then get you started—no matter how small your living space.

Diagonally laid bricks make up the beds in this beautiful suburban veggie garden from Suburban Existence.

Gorgeous heads of cabbage are grown by Cuban Gardener in 5-gallon buckets on a backyard patio.

◀

A stunning mixture of edibles and ornamentals is growing on the rooftop of Jeannie Phan's (@studioplants) apartment.

Epic Gardening reader Betsy Kurcinka set up simple raised beds to line the perimeter of her suburban backyard.

Katrina Kennedy repurposed old playground equipment as a sturdy trellis for an abundant crop of squash.

Squash hangs on an angled trellis in Katrina Kennedy's backyard.

Urban gardening doesn't have to be complex; repurposed Mason jars make excellent planters for kitchen salad greens.

A balcony has been turned into an edible urban paradise by Lisa Maria Trauer.

▶ For the space-challenged, vertical leafy green or herb walls are an incredible way to squeeze production out of tiny spaces.

A simple cluster of herbs in pots is enough to supply most kitchen gardeners with fresh herbs year-round.

Kathy from Eco Garden Systems shows off her standing patio garden filled with herbs and vegetables.

Ariel from *Zesty and Spicy* has turned her balcony into a productive rare herbs and vegetables "machine," with purple shiso, heirloom tomatoes, and more.

You can repurpose *anything* into an urban veggie planter—even an old porcelain toilet.

Aside from composting, some food scraps can even be used as planters themselves.

This urban garden uses pedal power to irrigate all of these containers.

Larger urban rooftops are ripe for transformation into raised-bed edible veggie gardens.

1

Getting Started

I know you're tempted to dive right into the garden plans. And if you're an experienced gardener, be my guest. But for new gardeners, or anyone in need of a brush up, check out this chapter, in which you'll learn:

- **How to audit your living space and select the right methods for you**
- **How plants use light, water, air, and nutrients**

- **Epic DIY soil mixes to fit any budget**
- **Whether you should start seeds or buy transplants**

Understanding these foundational principles will help you be a better gardener from the very beginning. So let's get started.

Creative use of limited space is the key to apartment gardening.

What Kind of Home Do You Live In?

To some degree, where you live will determine the limits of what you can grow. If you're living in a cozy apartment in the middle of the city, you have fewer growing options than if you're living in a single-family home in the suburbs. Don't be discouraged, though. You have *fewer* options, but you do have options.

Apartments and Condos

If you're living in a small apartment or condo, don't despair. There's *plenty* you can grow. The key to gardening in these spaces is making the best use of the limited space you have. Restrictions breed creativity, and I've found some of the most innovative gardening methods are ones created by apartment and condo gardeners.

RECOMMENDED METHODS
- vertical gardening
- balcony and patio gardening
- indoor edibles
- hydroponics

Growing vertically using rain gutters, hanging baskets, and balcony railings are all wonderful ways to squeeze delicious harvests (and beautiful plants) out of your space. If you're adventurous, you can even set up hydroponic systems that allow you to grow just about anything you could grow outdoors in a raised bed.

Townhomes

Townhomes offer slightly more space, and thus, more options. A typical townhome is multilevel and connected to another unit on at least one side, so you're still not completely free when it comes to outdoor growing space.

However, most townhomes have larger front and back patios, which means you can experiment with growing methods that require a bit more space. These include container gardening and raised bed gardening.

Both of these methods allow you to grow just about anything you'd normally grow in the ground and are often easier to maintain. You'll have fewer pest and disease issues and more control over your growing environment, which means larger, healthier harvests for you.

Single-Family Homes

Finally, we get to the single-family home. Houses are the big kahuna of gardening spaces for most urban dwellers and offers the most flexibility as far as space and growing methods.

All of the methods I'll cover in this book are available to you if you're living in a single-family home, but I recommend picking and choosing carefully because it's easy to be overwhelmed when starting out. Pick one or two growing methods and dive in deep instead of experimenting with all of them. You'll have better results, and you can always add more methods as you gain growing experience.

Some of the most productive gardens are born from small rooftops.

Yard space offers a wealth of options for the small-space urban gardener, such as a classic raised bed garden.

Homeowners' associations can be a thorn in your side when it comes to growing food at home.

Urban Gardening Regulations

Like any budding movement, urban gardening is facing its fair share of growing pains. Because cities, homeowners' associations (HOAs), and even our neighbors are used to urban landscapes looking a certain way, it's not uncommon to run into issues when you try to start growing your own food at home.

Zoning Laws

The zoning of your property will dictate what you're allowed to do on it gardening-wise. Most of you reading this book will be within a residential zone, which is typically the most restrictive when it comes to urban agriculture.

If you're gardening in your yard for your own personal use (or even giving away produce to family and friends), you usually won't run into a zoning issue. If your garden starts to look like a commercial operation, however, zoning issues might come up.

Unfortunately, there's no cut-and-dried answer when it comes to zoning. Every city has different rules, sometimes down to the type of residential zoning. I encourage you to look up your city's General Plan or check out online resources for your city ordinances.

Even if you do this, the answer is still somewhat unclear. Local ordinances aren't very clear on what you can and cannot do on your property. While I recommend you give your local ordinances a read-through, in the end it often comes down to common sense. If you're growing food for yourself and friends and not being a nuisance while you do it, you should be good to grow.

Homeowners' Associations

If you live in a residence that is governed by a homeowners' association, you may be frustrated to find that the regulations ban you from using your home to grow food, even if it's for personal consumption.

You'll know if you're allowed to grow food on your property by reading through the Declaration of Covenants, Conditions and Restrictions (CC&Rs). The CC&Rs outline what you can and cannot do with your property, along with the punishments for breaking the rules.

Here are a few common situations to look for in the covenants and rules that may prohibit front-yard urban gardening:

- restricts business activities
- prohibits agricultural use of your yard
- sets appearance standards for a yard, such as requiring a lawn

If you see one of these types of rules in your CC&Rs, don't despair. There are a few ways you can get around it. For instance, in California, homeowners' associations are prohibited from making rules that prevent a homeowner from planting plants with low water requirements. Although most veggies wouldn't be classified as low-water plants, there are certainly some that are, such as:

- beans
- peppers
- okra

Boulevard gardens are very popular and make sense, but not every municipality allows them. At the very least, you may find that there are restrictions on plant height, especially for corner lots.

On top of that, courts often don't enforce rules and covenants put in place by homeowners' associations if they conflict with public policy. As of right now, it's unclear whether "growing food" is a right or a matter of public policy, which is a shame. Let's hope this changes in the future.

In the end, if you're living in a property that's governed by an HOA, make sure you read the CC&Rs carefully and weigh the risk of growing in a way that might violate the rules.

Shining a light on would-be thieves is often enough to prevent your produce from being snatched.

Protecting Your Garden

It's a sad reality, but gardens can often be the target of passersby looking for some free produce. Most of my neighbors admire my garden and take the time to point it out as they walk past, but every so often I catch someone stealing a tomato or pepper that I've put months of effort into growing. It's frustrating, to say the least, so here are some of my strategies for preventing theft from two-legged garden predators.

Light Up Your Garden

Most theft or vandalism takes place under cover of darkness. Pick up some outdoor solar lights and install a few of them throughout your garden to illuminate it at night. I've found simply being visible discourages many would-be thieves.

Install Fencing

It may seem extreme, but if your garden is accessible from the sidewalk without a physical barrier, erecting one will drastically reduce theft and vandalism. Get creative with your fencing. Here are a few ideas for you:

- Bamboo fencing is inexpensive and attractive.
- Old logs lining your garden discourage foot traffic.
- Cages and trellises act as support for your plants and a passive barrier to passersby.

Put Up a Sign

Sometimes all it takes is a little human touch to discourage theft or vandalism. Putting up a simple sign that politely asks passersby to "Look, but not touch" is all you need. Nongardeners are often unaware of the time and love that goes into caring for plants and they may not realize the damage they're causing by messing with your garden.

Fencing is an aesthetically pleasing way to discourage garden thievery.

NO PICKING PLEASE

Nongardeners often don't know how much effort goes into growing plants. A sign can help get the point across.

Learning some basic gardening knowledge will help you start off strong, like healthy seedlings.

Green Thumb Basics

Before I get into the nitty-gritty details of urban gardening methods, it's important to understand *some* of the basics of growing plants. If you're already an experienced gardener, feel free to skip this section, although a refresher course never hurts. If you're new to growing plants or are a self-proclaimed "brown thumb," read this section carefully.

Instead of only giving you step-by-step information, I want you to "see behind the curtain" and truly understand how plants grow. If you understand the *why*, it'll be easier for you to come up with the *how* as you grow as a gardener.

How to Know What to Plant . . . and When to Plant It

The question I've been asked the most often over the years is, "What should I plant, and when should I plant it?"

Those are great questions. Without knowing the answers, you can't even begin to grow anything. You'll end up planting plants that aren't suited for your region or for the season, and your results will be disappointing.

As you might imagine, not all climates are created equal. In San Diego, where I live, the climate is sunny and temperate for most of the year. Sounds great, right? In theory, yes, but there are also some downsides. During unusually hot winters, I'll have a hard time growing veggies that are classic winter crops, such as broccoli and cauliflower. The temperatures are simply too high for those plants to form a tight, compact head.

While I may have a year-round growing season in my area, it comes at the cost of not being able to grow certain crops that actually prefer a cold season.

The takeaway here is that where you live in large part dictates *what you can grow*. In the United States, geographic regions are broken down into USDA Plant Hardiness Zones. Zones are split up by 10°F differences in their average annual minimum temperature. Lower numbers have lower minimum temperatures, and higher numbers have higher minimum temperatures.

The system gets a bit more complex with the addition of "a" and "b" subsections in each zone, representing 5°F differences in average annual minimum temperatures. For example, Zone 5a has an average annual minimum temperature of -20°F to -15°F, while Zone 10b (my zone) has an average annual minimum temperature of 35°F to 40°F.

To further complicate the matter, each hardiness zone has "first and last frost dates." These dates refer to the first and last days that you'll have killing frosts, on average, in your region. The terminology is a *bit* confusing, however.

- The *first* day you can plant *in* the ground is equal to your *last* frost date.
- The *last* day you can harvest your crops is equal to your *first* frost date.

To start with, look up your USDA Plant Hardiness Zone (planthardiness.ars.usda.gov) online to get a sense of your growing season. For example, if you live in Zone 6, your last frost is usually March 16 to 30 and your first frost is usually November 1 to 15, giving you an eight-month growing season.

WHAT TO DO ONCE YOU KNOW YOUR HARDINESS ZONE

The most important thing to know about your zone is this: **It's just a general guideline.** Zones don't take into account your local conditions. All they do is help you figure out the "bookends" of when you can and cannot garden in your region.

Later on, I'll discuss *microclimates* and *crop protection* in order to extend your growing season and grow crops that you "shouldn't" be able to grow in your zone.

Hardiness Zones and Their Frost Dates

Zone*	Last Frost Date	First Frost Date
1	June 1–30	July 1–31
2	May 16–31	Aug 6–31
3	May 11–25	Sept 1–30
4	April 16–30	Oct 1–15
5	April 1–15	Oct 16–31
6	Mar 16–30	Nov 1–15
7	Mar 1–15	Nov 16–30
8	Feb 1–28	Dec 1–15
9	Jan 1–30	Dec 16–31
10	Rare or never	Rare or never

* Please note: Due to the extremely difficult growing seasons of the zones at the extremes, as well as the fact that few people live in these climates, I have omitted Zones 11 and 12.

GROWING OUTSIDE OF THE USA?

The important takeaway from this hardiness zone section is that your climate will determine if you can grow a plant in your region—*and* when you can grow it. But what if you're living outside of the United States? My number one tip would be to consult local resources to see if there's an equivalent of the USDA system in your country. However, if you're up for a little online searching, you may be able to find this information yourself—the USDA system has been mapped to most countries on Earth.

Here are a few additional resources for you:

- **Australia:** Australia lies in zones 7 through 12, according to the USDA system, although the Australian National Botanic Gardens have created their own adaptation which you can view online.
- **Canada:** The government of Canada has put together a similar system called the Plant Hardiness Zones of Canada, which you can look at online.
- **United Kingdom:** The Royal Horticultural Society has a system ranging from H1a (Zone 13 equivalent) to H7 (Zone 5 equivalent). Most of the United Kingdom is within Zones 8 to 10 on the USDA scale.

Understanding how plants use light is crucial to a healthy, happy harvest.

What Plants Need to Survive

Plants are similar to us in terms of what they require to live, such as:

- light
- water
- air
- nutrients
- environment

Over millions of years, certain plants have adapted to specific geographic or environmental areas, meaning they require different amounts of each of these fundamental ingredients. Many beginning gardeners go wrong by giving all of their plants *exactly* the same growing conditions.

As a gardener, you must remember that you're growing plants outside of their natural environment. You have to give your plants the growing conditions they're used to if you want them to thrive.

LIGHT

Do you remember learning about photosynthesis in school (but maybe not making too much sense of it)? It's probably due to the fact that it looked like this:

$$6H_2O + 6CO_2 \rightarrow C_6H_{12}O_6 + 6O_2$$

That's a lot of numbers and letters if you ask me. Here's a simpler explanation:

Plants use light, water, and carbon dioxide to make sugar, which is converted into ATP (the stuff that fuels all living things) during cellular respiration.

As long as you give your plants light, they'll grow just fine, right? Not quite. The quality, quantity, and duration of light your plants receive drastically affects their growth rate.

QUALITY

One glance at a gorgeous rainbow and it's clear that "white" light is composed of different colors. What if I told you that your precious plants have an appetite for specific colors of light more than others?

When we talk about light as gardeners, we are most interested in the range of light known as *photosynthetically active radiation*. This is the range between 400 to 735 nanometers, encompassing the full spectrum of visible light.

Plants love light in the purple/blue (400 to 490 nanometers) range early in their life, when they're putting out lots of branches and leaves. As they move toward flowering and fruiting, they require more yellow, orange, and red light (580 to 735 nanometers) range.

If you're growing outdoors, this progression happens naturally over the course of a season, so you don't need to worry about it too much. However, if space is limited and you're growing indoors under lights, you'll need to adjust the color temperature of the lights under which you're growing. I'll get deeper into this in the hydroponics chapter.

QUANTITY

Now that we know the spectrum of light plants prefer, we need to look at *how much* of that light they want. Whether you're growing outdoors under the sun or indoors under grow lights, there are two acronyms to understand:

- **PPF (Photosynthetic Photon Flux):** How much light is emitted per second by a light source
- **PPFD (Photosynthetic Photon Flux Density):** How many photons are delivered per second over a meter squared, at a specific distance

I know this sounds intense, but it's very important to understand as far as how plants use light. Think of light as billions of little raindrops hitting the surface of your plant's leaves. When talking about the quantity of light, *this* is what we mean. How densely packed are the photons that the plant is using during the process of photosynthesis?

Growing outdoors has its challenges. Shade, overcast days, or a neighbor's tree blocking your property can all get in the way of providing enough light to your plants. Many gardeners opt to grow indoors because they can more finely control the amount of light they give their plants.

If you're planning to start your gardening adventure outdoors, don't fear. In later chapters, I'll get into where you should locate your garden to take full advantage of the sun.

DURATION

Some plants like a bit more light than others. Some have crucial processes that can only take place when it's dark. Others still can be run under twenty-four-hour grow lights and grow vigorously. The most important thing to know about your plants and light is how much they want in a given day. Usually this is given in a number of hours per day, but if you want to get nerdy, what we're really talking about is the *daily light integral*.

Wave Length in Nanometers

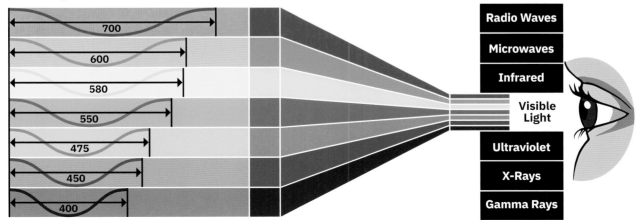

Plants mainly use light in the visible range of 400 to 735 nanometers.

This is a picture-perfect demonstration of the proper hand-watering technique.

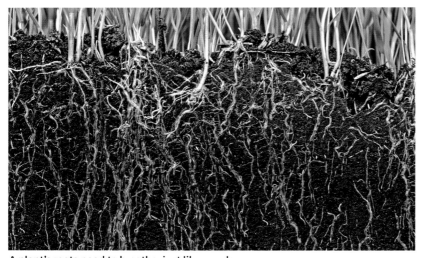
A plant's roots need to breathe, just like you do.

A good rule of thumb is to check the soil daily when first starting out. Put a finger a few inches into the soil and check for moisture. Generally speaking, plants need water when the soil is dry about 2 to 3 inches deep. Over time you'll develop a sense for watering, but at the beginning it's better to over-check than undercheck.

AIR
If you think of photosynthesis as a manufacturing process, one of the raw inputs is carbon dioxide. And where is carbon dioxide found in abundance, especially in modern times? In the air. Plants take in carbon dioxide via their *stomata* and use it in many life processes.

There's another part of a plant that loves air, which is a plant's root system. Roots love oxygen, as it allows them to collect both water and nutrients from the soil. You might be surprised to know that a plant can actually drown if the roots aren't given enough oxygen. I'll get more into how to avoid that in the soil section.

What about wind? Wind can either be a great benefit or a bane to your plants. Wind helps cool plants down, reduces the occurrences of fungal diseases, and strengthens a plant's structure. At the same time, too much wind can dry a plant out too much, throw weed seeds everywhere, or even break stems.

The daily light integral is the amount of light that a particular plant can accumulate in a twenty-four-hour period. The DLI, which I'll refer to in colloquial terms as a number of hours of light per day, will depend on both where the plant naturally evolved, as well as the developmental stage that plant is in. For example, spinach can get away with about four to five hours of light per day while tomatoes suck up at least eight hours.

WATER
Like us, plants are mostly water. In fact, the aptly named watermelon is 92 percent water. For reference, you and I are only around 60 percent water.

Water is used in nearly every process a plant undergoes, from photosynthesis to remaining stiff and upright. For now, all you need to know about water is that having too much or too little of it is the number-one problem most new gardeners face.

Top-dressing a garden bed with granular organic fertilizer.

ENVIRONMENT

Depending on the plant, there will be a range of temperatures to which it is acclimated. If it can survive in a colder climate, we call it a "cold-hardy" plant. If it's able to survive in warmer climates, it's heat tolerant. As you build a familiarity with certain crops and the environmental conditions they love, you can start planting them strategically in different parts of your garden. For instance, you can squeeze a few spinach plants into a spot that gets the first bit of shade in the afternoon, as it's one of the most shade- and cold-tolerant greens. On the other hand, if you have a section that's absolutely blasted by the sun all day long, it might be a good spot to sow some okra.

Your plant's environment also includes factors such as wind stress, humidity, proximity to other beneficial plants, and overall location in your garden or home.

These urban gardening nuances will come with practice and understanding. And speaking of understanding, it's time to get into one of the most important elements in gardening . . . your soil.

NUTRIENTS

Plants need nutrients in order to support their growth. In fact, there are seventeen different macro- and micronutrients plants need in order to thrive.

Of these, the "Big 3" are *nitrogen, phosphorus,* and *potassium.* You might be more familiar with these as NPK, often displayed as three numbers on a bag of fertilizer, such as "3-5-3." While N, P, and K are the dominant nutrients used by plants, there are more "forgotten soldiers" that plants also need in order to grow well.

From water and air, they obtain:
- Carbon
- Hydrogen
- Oxygen

From the soil, they get:
- Calcium
- Magnesium
- Sulfur
- Iron
- Molybdenum
- Boron
- Copper
- Manganese
- Sodium
- Zinc
- Nickel
- Chlorine
- Cobalt
- Aluminum
- Silicon
- Vanadium
- Selenium

The presence of earthworms is a fantastic sign of healthy soil.

WHAT'S IN SOIL?

First, let's talk about soil types. Soil is mostly made up of these three different types of particles: sand, silt, and clay. Certain types of soil are better than others for growing plants.

Clay particles are the smallest, then silt, and then sand. When soil is exclusively made up of one type of particle, you've got a recipe for bad soil. Your soil might have poor aeration, retain too much water, be prone to compaction . . . the list goes on.

In the perfect garden, sand, silt, clay, and organic matter are balanced to form a type of soil called "loam," which is well draining, nutrient rich, and retains enough water for plants to use. In short, loamy soil is the "holy grail" when it comes to growing plants.

Soil: The Bedrock of Your Garden

Although we walk over it every day, most of us pay little attention to the world beneath our feet. Soil is a curious thing; it's composed of organic matter, minerals, liquids, gases, and living things, all of which combine to support much of the life on our humble planet.

Entire books could be (and have) been written about soil, but for an urban gardener there are a few key concepts to understand to make your life much easier. When talking about soil as a gardener, be concerned with these three things:

- the soil type
- the nutrient contents of the soil
- the biological life within the soil

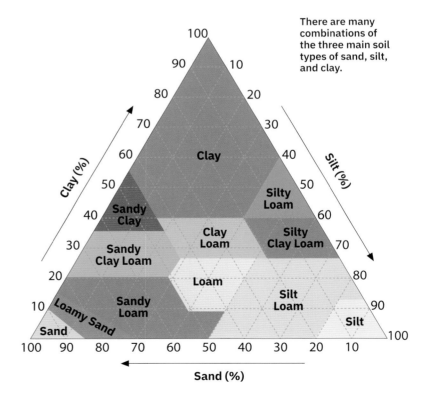

There are many combinations of the three main soil types of sand, silt, and clay.

Loamy soil is what we're shooting for when making soil mixes for our gardens.

However, most of us aren't blessed with loamy soil . . . at least not when we begin our gardening journey. We might also be growing in containers, so we have to create the perfect soil from scratch. This might sound like a daunting task, but later in this section I'll go over a few easy soil recipes you can make at home.

Loam
- **Weight**: medium
- **Nutrients**: medium–high
- **Drainage**: medium
- **Other**: a mixture of sand, silt, and clay

The classic definition of loamy soil is 40 percent sand, 40 percent silt, and 20 percent clay. This ratio can shift toward any of the three, creating subtypes such as sandy loam, silty loam, clay loam, and so on. What's important to know about loamy soil is that it has the benefits of each type of soil particle without too many of the downsides. It contains a high amount of nutrients, holds on to moisture (but not too much), and has enough space between the particles for air and microorganisms to thrive.

Large grained and well draining, sandy soils often need a healthy dose of amendments.

Now let's take a look at the characteristics of the three types of soil textures.

Sandy
- **Weight**: light
- **Nutrients**: low
- **Drainage**: very high
- **Other**: warms easily and is acidic

Sandy soils are dominated by large particles, making them porous, well draining, and poor at holding water. They're usually deficient in nutrients, as these large sandy particles typically aren't comprised of organic matter.

Improving Sandy Soil
- Add 3 to 4 inches of finished compost or well-rotted manure.
- Add 1 inch of leaves, grass clippings, bark, or other organic mulch to retain moisture.
- Add 2 inches of organic matter per year.

Silt
- **Weight**: light
- **Nutrients**: medium–high
- **Drainage**: medium
- **Other**: compacts and washes away easily

Silty soils have a bit more clay than sandy soil, but not much. A typical silty soil will contain less than 10 percent clay content. This makes it susceptible to compacting, leaving no space for air and water to penetrate the soil.

Improving Silty Soil
- Add a 1-inch layer of organic matter per year.
- Keep an eye on the surface of the soil to watch for crusting.
- Avoid walking on the soil's surface to minimize compaction.

Silt-dominant soils often need a bit of compost to make them garden-ready.

Heavy clay soil is one of the hardest types to work with in the garden.

Clay

- **Weight**: heavy
- **Nutrients**: high
- **Drainage**: low
- **Other**: dries and cakes easily

Clay soil is a bit more complex because there are a few variations. You can have light (10 to 25 percent), medium (25 to 40 percent), or heavy (>40 percent) clay soil. Each of these types has slightly different qualities to them.

Light clay soil is at high risk of developing a "cake" or "crust" when it dries. It'll often become very hard as it dries out, needing to be broken up by hand or power tools.

Medium clay soil is darker in appearance than light clay and has a better ability to resist crusting and caking over. It also has a decent ability to transport water and air to roots. However, if conditions are too dry or too wet, it can still run into issues with texture.

Heavy clay soil is one of the best at holding on to water, but this isn't necessarily a good thing. Plants often have a hard time accessing this water, as it's tightly bound in the soil. If overwatered, heavy clay soil will take on a puttylike texture and drown out plant roots.

Improving Clay Soil

- Work 2 to 3 inches of organic matter into the surface of the soil to loosen it.
- Use permanent raised beds for improved drainage.
- Avoid stepping on the soil to minimize compaction.

Extremely clayey, heavy soil will ball together when a handful is squeezed and have a smooth texture.

Loamy soil will hold its form a bit, but crumble and break slightly—exactly what we want.

SIMPLE SOIL TESTS TO DETERMINE YOUR SOIL TYPE

Now that you have a good understanding of the structure of soil, let's figure out what type you have at home.

The Squeeze Test

Take a handful of moist (but not wet) soil from your garden and squeeze tightly. Open your hand and see what happened to the soil.

- It holds its shape until you poke it; then it crumbles. Congratulations, you have loamy soil.
- It holds its shape, even when poked. This is a sign you have clay soil.
- It breaks apart as soon as you open your hand. You likely have sandy or silty soil.

The Mason Jar Test

The Mason jar test is a simple way to check your soil's structure on the cheap.

Fill a clean Mason jar halfway with a sample of soil from your garden. It's a good idea to use soil from a few different areas to get a good representation of overall soil quality.

Fill the rest of the jar with water, leaving about 1 inch of room at the top. Screw on the lid and shake vigorously for at least one minute to mix the soil.

Set the jar on a flat surface for at least a day to let the particles settle. After some time sitting still, the particles in your soil will separate into these different layers:

- Sand, rocks, and other large particles will be at the bottom of the jar.
- Silty particles will be in the middle.
- Clay particles will slowly settle at the top of the soil.

Now you can make a rough estimate of how much of each type of particle you have in your soil overall. Remember, the ideal soil is loamy at around 40 percent sand, 40 percent silt, and 20 percent clay.

The Drainage Test

While the squeeze test will give you a good idea of your soil's ability to retain water, there's a better way to measure drainage.

- Dig a hole 1 foot deep and 6 inches wide.
- Fill the hole with water.
- Keep track of how long it takes for the hole to drain fully.

If this process takes more than four hours, your soil has poor drainage.

Make sure you use soil from multiple areas of the garden for a representative sample.

The soil and water mixture before shaking

Three different soil samples after settling for 72 hours

University of Minnesota
Soil Testing Laboratory

SOIL TEST REPORT
Lawn and Garden

Client Copy
Department of Soil, Water, and Climate
Minnesota Extension Service
Agricultural Experiment Station

Page	1
Report No.	58014
Laboratory No.	120493
Date Received	04/09/14
Date Reported	04/14/14

Sample/Field Number: MARK

SOIL TEST RESULTS

Estimated Soil Texture	Organic Matter %	Soluble Salts mmhos/cm	pH	Buffer Index	Nitrate NO3-N ppm	Olsen Phosphorus ppm P	Bray 1 Phosphorus ppm P	Potassium ppm K	Buffer SO4 -S ppm	Zinc ppm	Iron ppm	Manganese ppm	Copper ppm	Boron ppm	Calcium ppm	Magnesium ppm	Lead ppm
Medium	8.3		7.2				100+	188									

INTERPRETATION OF SOIL TEST RESULTS

Phosphorus (P) PPPPPPPPPPPPPPPPPPPPPPPPPPPPPPPPPPPF

5	10	15	20	25
Low	Medium	High	V. High	

Potassium (K) KKKKKKKKKKKKKKKKKKKKKKKKKKK

25	75	125	175	225
Low	Medium	High	V. High	

pH **
3.0	4.0	5.0	6.0	7.0	8.0	9.0
Acid		Optimum			Alkaline	

Soluble Salts
| 0 | 1.0 | 2.0 | 3.0 | 4.0 | 5.0 | 6.0 | 7.0 | 8.0 | 9.0 | 10.0 |
| Satisfactory | | Possible Problem | | | Excessive Salts | |

RECOMMENDATIONS FOR: Vegetable garden

LIME RECOMMENDATION: 0 LBS/100 SQ.FT.
TOTAL AMOUNT OF EACH NUTRIENT TO APPLY PER YEAR:*

NITROGEN	PHOSPHATE	POTASH
0.15 LBS/100 SQ.FT.	0 LBS/100 SQ.FT.	0.1 LBS/100 SQ.FT.

THE APPROXIMATE RATIO OR PROPORTION OF THESE NUTRIENTS IS: 30-0-20

Use a fertilizer with the percentage of nutrients closest to the above ratio. Apply according to the instructions on the fertilizer bag or container, or determine the amount required from the instructions given on the back side of this report. Since meeting the exact amount required for each nutrient will not be possible in most cases, it is more important to apply the amount of nitrogen required and compromise some for phosphate and potash.

If a fertilizer contains phosphate and/or potash, it can be mixed in the spring or fall into the top 4-6 inches of topsoil. If a fertilizer containing only nitrogen is used, it should be applied in the spring, tilling or raking it into the surface. Nitrogen is easily leached through soil.

For sweetcorn, tomatoes, cabbage, and vine crops such as squash and cucumbers, an additional application of 1/6 lb. nitrogen per 100 sq. ft. may be desirable at midseason. This can be accomplished by applying 1/2 lb. (about one cup) of 34-0-0 fertilizer. Throughly water fertilizer into the soil.

A good soil-testing lab will send back a detailed report along with suggested changes to make to your soil.

Soil samples have been laid out for laboratory testing.

Soil-testing labs will take your sample and send back a report with the pH, texture, nutrient density, and recommendations on how to correct any soil issues. This is one of the absolute best ways to know *exactly* what's going on in your soil.

WHAT ELSE IS IN SOIL?

If you were reading carefully in the soil texture section, you'll notice I said soil is *mostly* sand, silt, and clay particles. That's because soil also contains air, water, decomposed organic matter, and living organisms. Your soil is truly a smorgasbord of ingredients that all work together to support the plants we grow in our gardens.

Air

Plants need to breathe, just like us. A plant's roots seek out air pockets in soil for precious oxygen. If you have compacted soil, your plants will suffocate and die.

Water

Water is essential not only as a raw ingredient for your plant's growth but also to give the microorganisms and worms in your soil something to drink. As long as your soil holds on to enough water (but not too much), you've got nothing to worry about.

Organic Matter

Organic matter is a crucial component of soil, as it feeds all of the living organisms in your soil, which break it down into its constituent parts and thus make nutrients available for your plants. The best way to think of organic matter in gardening terms is as a "slow-release" fertilizer. It's slow release because it takes *time* for those organisms to break it down.

SHOULD YOU GET A PROFESSIONAL SOIL TEST?

If you're serious about your soil and want all of the information your heart could ever desire, consider ordering a soil test. Most local nurseries and garden centers have a connection to a soil lab. You can also contact your county's local Extension office. They're well connected with universities and other resources to help troubleshoot your soil.

The key to a good soil test is collecting your soil properly. As a general rule, dig at a depth of around 6 to 8 inches and collect soil from one side of the hole. Add this soil to a bucket, then move around your yard and collect soil from a few other spots in your garden to make sure you have a well-rounded sample.

Living Organisms

Healthy soil is full of millions of different organisms, all of which have their own place in the "soil food web." By cultivating healthy soil, you're also cultivating the entire ecosystem within the soil, which in turn pays you back by giving you strong, healthy, and productive plants.

MAKING SUCCESSFUL SOIL MIXES

Now that you've got a solid understanding of how soil works, it's time to build your own soil mix. There are plenty of different recipes out there, each with its own take on the "best" soil mix.

The truth is simple: the best soil mix will be tailored to your unique growing situation. Every soil mix needs a combination of these three qualities:

- aeration and drainage
- water retention
- nutrients

The ingredients you use to get the job done will depend heavily on where you live and what you have access to. That being said, shoot for a 1:1:1 ratio of each of these soil qualities, and you'll be off to a great start.

Earthworms are one of the most recognizable organisms living in healthy soil.

An assortment of soil amendments is used for DIY soil mixes.

Clockwise from the top are peat moss, perlite, compost, organic fertilizer, and worm castings.

Mix well, adding water to moisten as you go.

The final Raised Bed Mix.

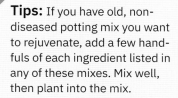

Tips: If you have old, non-diseased potting mix you want to rejuvenate, add a few hand-fuls of each ingredient listed in any of these mixes. Mix well, then plant into the mix.

Use a tarp or wheelbarrow to keep things tidy and also to adequately mix all components of your soil mix. Then, transfer the mix into your container or bed.

When adding organic amend-ments to your soil, wait until the soil is in its final resting place. Work into the top 3 to 6 inches of soil, then water it well.

Raised Bed Mix

This mix is designed for raised beds, where the soil volume is a bit larger and you don't need to worry *as* much about water draining out of the soil. It's a well-balanced mix of commonly available ingredients. The soil amendments are up to you as well; the ones I recommend are what have worked for me over the years.

Ingredients
- 1 part perlite (for aeration and drainage)
- 1 part peat moss or coconut coir (for water retention)
- 1 part blended compost (for organic matter and nutrition)
- a sprinkling of Azomite, kelp meal, and worm tea (for micronutrients and inoculation with soil microorganisms)

The final Dirt Cheap Soil Mix won't break the bank.

Top row, left to right: compost, sand, topsoil; bottom row, left to right: organic fertilizer, worm castings

Top row, left to right: peat moss, perlite, compost; bottom row, left to right: worm castings, organic fertilizer

Dirt Cheap Soil Mix

If you can't find some of the materials in the Raised Bed Mix, or prefer to use less-expensive components, you can make a wonderful sandy loam mix using some cheaper inputs.

Ingredients
- 1 part screened topsoil
- 1 part builder's sand
- 1 part blended compost

These three ingredients alone will get you a nice sandy loam mix, which is pretty darn close to what you want in raised beds or containers. Better yet, all of these ingredients cost you nothing if you're resourceful. You can get topsoil from your yard, sand from a beach, and compost from your local municipality. If you want to reduce the chance of disease or weed seeds in your mix, go for bagged black dirt from a garden center as a replacement for topsoil. You can also make your own compost if you want extra sustainability points.

Because these materials are often cheap or free, sometimes the quality is low. I suggest double-checking your sources, as well as running the materials through a screen or sifter to remove rocks, bark, and large particles that will hinder your plants' roots.

The beauty of this mix is not only in the low cost, but the combination of soil particles and textures also create a mix that isn't going to become like cement in your beds. The mixture of textures allows good aeration and minimal compaction.

Potting Mix

A good potting mix is designed to retain a bit more water than a raised bed mix. The smaller the volume of soil you're growing in, the quicker it dries out, leaving your plants thirsty and suffering in the heat. For that reason, we need to bump up the water-retention qualities of our mix by including these components.

Ingredients
- 2 parts peat moss or coconut coir
- 1 part compost or well-rotted manure
- ½ part perlite, vermiculite, or pumice
- Optional: garden lime, dolomite, Epsom salts

Compost tumblers are a compact and efficient way to compost in urban spaces.

THE ABSOLUTE BASICS OF COMPOSTING

There are entire books on composting out there; this section is meant as a primer to pique your interest in the topic. The rules of composting are simple in practice but can be hard to perfect in the garden. Don't get discouraged if you run into trouble your first go around; it happens to everyone.

First, what do you add to your compost pile? Organic matter can be broken down into *browns* and *greens*, or materials that are high in carbon or nitrogen, respectively. The ratio you're shooting for in your compost pile is around 25 to 30 parts carbon to 1 part nitrogen.

If you have too much carbon, the process slows down. If you have too much nitrogen, your pile is often too moist and starts to smell bad.

However, don't think that you need to add thirty times more browns than you do greens to your pile . . . nothing could be further from the truth. Both browns and greens have individual carbon-to-nitrogen ratios; they're just named that because greens have lower ratios than browns.

Take a look at the following table to see what I mean. Eggshells come in at 10:1, while fresh garden waste is around 30:1. Pine needles are about 80:1, while newspaper is 175:1. Your goal when constructing a pile is to use ingredients that end up averaging to about 30:1; that's the sweet spot.

Integrating Composting into Your Urban Garden

It's completely fine to set up a garden without any composting system, especially if you're a beginner in the art of growing plants. However, if you want to dabble with one of the most powerful ways to add nutrients back into your soil, read on.

At its most simple, composting is the practice of throwing organic matter in a pile and letting it decompose. It happens in nature all the time, but under your watchful eye you can speed the process considerably.

Instead of tossing food scraps into the trash, turn them into rich, black compost.

Greens	Browns
Fresh grass clippings (17:1)	Dried leaves (70:1)
Eggshells (10:1)	Sawdust or small wood chips (500:1)
Coffee grounds (25:1)	Shredded newspaper (175:1)
Fresh garden waste (30:1)	Straw or hay (90:1)
Seaweed (19:1)	Pine needles (80:1)

After you concoct the perfect mixture of browns and greens, it's time to add them to your pile. It's a good idea to layer these in alternating layers to ensure no part of the pile is overly saturated with one type of material.

Tip: The smaller the pieces you add to your compost pile, the quicker they'll break down. The increased surface area created by shredding your materials makes it easier for microbes to munch on them.

After you've added materials to your pile, there are three factors that you need to keep in mind:

- **Temperature**—A good, active compost pile will be in the 140 to 160°F range. This is hot enough to break down organic matter, but not so hot that the microbes will die off.
- **Airflow**—Good aeration encourages growth of aerobic microbes, the ones we want breaking down our pile. Too little aeration encourages anaerobic bacteria, causing your pile to putrefy and smell terrible.
- **Moisture**—Your pile should feel moist but not wet. If you pick up a handful of compost, it should feel about as moist as a squeezed-out sponge.

FIXING THE MOST COMMON COMPOSTING PROBLEMS

Creating quality compost can be a finicky process. At any point, your pile can get thrown off balance. If you run into an issue in your own compost, consult this table for a quick troubleshooting. These are the most common issues I run into in my own compost piles.

Problem	Solution
The pile is dry and not heating up.	The pile needs more water, which you can add by adding more green material or watering until the pile is slightly moist when squeezed between your hands.
The pile is wet and not heating up.	Heat buildup is triggered by volume. You usually need about 1 cubic yard of material before your pile will sustain heat. Add more material to your pile.
The pile is large, wet, and not heating up.	Add more green materials to your pile and turn it with a fork or shovel to increase aeration.
The pile doesn't stay hot long enough.	Turn your compost pile, taking care to move material from the center to the outside.
The pile is wet and smells awful.	Add more brown material and turn your pile.
Nothing is breaking down.	Add more green materials and water; then turn the pile to mix well.
The layers are matted and not breaking down.	Don't add large amounts of the same type of material to the same layer. Break up matted material and chop large pieces down to size; then turn the pile.

THE THREE MAIN COMPOSTING TECHNIQUES

There are a few different approaches to composting, each with its own unique set of ups and downs. Whichever you choose will depend on how adventurous you are as well as how much space you can dedicate to a composting system.

Hot Composting

In urban environments, tumbler composters make better use of space and can crank out compost at a faster pace. They're easy to aerate and fill due to their spinning design and work well if you put in finely shredded green and brown organic matter. If properly managed, you can create compost in as little as three to four weeks.

Bokashi Composting

The Bokashi method is an anaerobic method of composting, meaning it doesn't require oxygen to function well. All you need to do is place your food scraps into an airtight bucket and layer with Bokashi bran, which is bran that been inoculated with specific microbes that will start to decompose and ferment food scraps.

Once your scraps have been fermented, you can either mix them into your soil or toss them into your compost tumbler to finish them off. One important note with the Bokashi method is that the finished product isn't actually *finished compost*. However, the fermentation process makes the final breaking down process much faster.

Hot composting in a bin is one of the most tried-and-true methods available to you. It typically uses three different bins to move compost through stages of decomposition. You can also use a single-bin system and let your compost go through the process without moving it.

For ease of use and faster turnaround times, consider a compost tumbler.

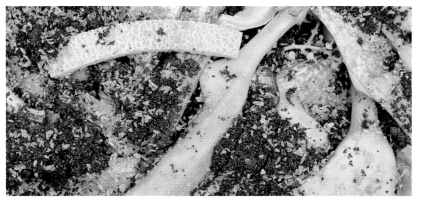

This is a good example of pre-compost fermented via the Bokashi method.

Worm Composting

Vermicomposting is, hands down, my favorite method of composting in an urban environment. It's one of the fastest methods due to using worms to break down food scraps and brown waste. On top of that, it's great for smaller composting operations, which is perfect for urban gardeners like you and me.

If you're going to experiment with worm composting, you don't need to break the bank with fancy systems. A large storage tote with some holes drilled into the sides and top will do.

Red wigglers are the best types of worms for vermicomposting. They make short work of food scraps, as just 2,000 worms can eat up to 1 pound per day of food waste. They'll double their population every three months, but they are also a self-regulating organism, meaning they won't reproduce much if there aren't enough resources for their offspring.

While worms love to munch on food scraps, there are a few types of food you *shouldn't* add to your bin. These foods will alter the pH of your bin too much or irritate the worms as they move throughout the bin:

- meats, bones, or any fats and oils
- any dairy products (crushed eggshells are okay)
- canned and/or processed foods
- citrus
- onions or garlic
- anything spicy
- soap
- glossy paper products or ones with colored ink
- poisonous plants
- garden waste treated with pesticides

Worms make quick work of almost all food scraps coming out of your kitchen.

You can get started with worm composting using a simple storage tote.

The worm composting process is a bit different from traditional composting because you're using such large organisms to break down waste compared to microbial activity of classic composting. You have to layer worm bins with bedding for the worms; shredded newspaper and sawdust are a fantastic bedding mixture. Then layer food scraps and more bedding until your bin is full, taking care to keep your bin nice and moist with good airflow.

Separating Worms from Their Castings

If you've done your job, the worms should be turning their bedding and food scraps into dark-colored, nutrient-rich worm castings, also known as "black gold." Before you can use these castings, you have to get your worms *out* of them so you can put them to work on another batch of food scraps.

Here are two different tried-and-true methods for harvesting your worm castings:

1 Move finished castings to one side of your bin and food scraps to the other. Worms will naturally migrate to the food.
2 Place another bin on top of your existing bin with holes drilled in the bottom, then fill the new bin with bedding and food scraps. Worms will migrate upward into the new bin, separating themselves from the castings.

OBSERVATION: The Ultimate Skill in the Garden

Gardening often has *nothing* to do with plants and everything to do with *you*. One of the most important skills to cultivate in the garden is your own attention and awareness.

I realize this sounds very "woo-woo." But by opening your eyes and noticing what's going on in your garden, you'll begin to really "see" what's happening with your plants and gain a deeper understanding of how to grow. You'll be able to develop these skills:

- Spot pest problems before they become full-blown infestations.
- See signs of disease before it's too late.
- Notice nutrient deficiencies before they get out of control.
- See how your plants react to their environments.

Paying attention in the garden is, hands down, the number one skill to practice. Plus, it's a meditative and peaceful way to grow. I find my time in the garden provides me a brief break from the modern world, even if it's only for twenty minutes a day.

Don't feel bad if you decide not to start seeds when you first start gardening.

An Age-Old Debate: Seeds vs. Transplants

I recommend that you as a beginner gardener buy seedlings from a local nursery and plant those. You might be wondering, "Isn't this cheating? Shouldn't I be growing all of my plants from seed?"

It's certainly an option, but there are a lot of things that can go wrong in the seed-starting process that will slow down your growing season. The last thing you want to happen is to start a few tomato seeds only to have them looking sickly (or dead) when it comes time to plant them in the garden. Then you miss your entire planting window for that crop.

Here are a few scenarios where buying seedlings from a nursery makes more sense than starting your plants from seed:

- you're just starting out in gardening
- you want to grow something that is harder to start from seed
- you want to grow a localized variety you can't find seeds for
- you need to get something planted ASAP and can't wait for seeds to germinate
- you want to "spot fill" empty sections in your garden with quick plantings

As you gain more experience in the garden, starting from seed becomes both easier and more enjoyable. There's a special satisfaction I get from slicing into a tomato that I put into the ground as a tiny seed just a few months before.

A SIMPLE SEED-STARTING PROCESS

If you *do* want to try your hand at starting your plants from seed, here's a foolproof process to follow. Keep in mind that young seedlings need a good amount of care at the beginning of their lives, so don't neglect them.

Before You Start

- Prepare for some losses by starting a few extra seeds per plant than you think you'll need.
- Read the seed packets carefully; some seeds must be soaked, scratched (nicked), or refrigerated before they will germinate successfully.
- Use clean containers to avoid contaminating your seedlings early on in their life.
- Label your containers with tape and markers or plant ID labels; there's nothing worse than forgetting what you planted.

Fill your containers with a potting mix made for seedlings. You can use equal parts of peat moss, perlite, and compost.

If you use regular potting soil, you may introduce contaminants and pathogens from the outdoors that will cause your seedlings to suffer from *damping off*, a nasty disease that rots seedlings right after they germinate. No fun.

Pour your mix into a bucket and moisten with warm water, then fill your containers to slightly below the top.

Plant your seeds based on the instructions on the back of the packet. The most important instruction to follow is planting depth, as some seeds need light to germinate and some must be buried pretty deep in order to sprout.

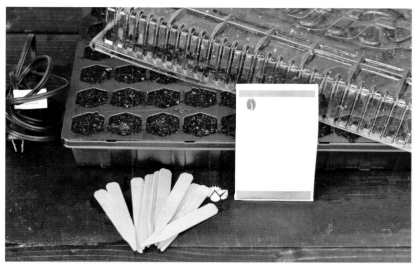

Grab a basic seed-starting kit from a home-and-garden store or scrounge up materials around the house; either works just fine.

Planting a couple of seeds per cell ensures at least one will germinate.

I highly recommend planting two or three seeds per hole to guarantee one of them successfully germinates.

A heat mat (under the seedling tray) and a humidity dome help cultivate the right germination environment.

Young seedlings reaching toward the light.

PREPARING YOUR SEEDLINGS FOR TRANSPLANTING

Congratulations, you've started your first batch of seeds. However, the job isn't done. These delicate seedlings have had a privileged upbringing indoors. If you were to bring them outdoors right away, they would perish, unused to the harsh conditions and climate change. You have to "harden them off" by doing the following:

- Water less often during the last week before you move your seedlings outdoors.
- A week before you transplant them into your outdoor garden, move your seedlings into dappled shade outside for a few hours a day. Gradually increase the number of hours per day.
- Keep the mix nice and moist during this entire process to prevent damage to the young seedlings.

Once your seedlings have hardened off, you're ready to transplant. If you think about it, you're now at the point in the growing process that you'd be at if you bought transplants from a nursery. Give yourself a pat on the back and get to planting.

Now that we've gotten the basics out of the way, let's get into how to grow plants, no matter how small your living space.

Cover your containers with a humidity dome. If you don't have a proper humidity dome, you can use a plastic bag with holes poked into it. Young seedlings need higher humidity and soil temperature (65° to 75°F) to germinate well, so place them in an area that gets a bit of warmth throughout the day.

As soon as you see seedlings start to pop out of the mix, remove the humidity dome and move your seedlings into bright light. Their leaves are hungry for light. Once you see their second set of leaves start developing, move seedlings into larger individual pots and water them in.

▶
Young celeriac transplants have been hardened off and are ready for transplanting.

2

Container Gardening

The simplest way to dip your toe into urban gardening is a bit of soil, a pot, and a seedling. My gardening journey began back in 2010 when I grew massive basil plants with my brother. We didn't have much space at the time but were still able to grow enough basil to have pesto for an entire summer . . . and then some.

The world of container gardening can be confusing, though. First of all, what type of container is best? Plastic planters, terra-cotta pots, glass? Each type of container has its own benefits, but the best containers have the right blend of these three qualities:

- **Volume**—They're the right size for the plants you're growing.
- **Material**—They're made out of the right material for your individual needs.
- **Drainage**—They let water drain out, reducing the risk of root rot.

Volume

Your first consideration is the size of your container. Different plants require different minimum sizes. As a general rule of thumb, bigger is better. Most veggies you'll grow in a container want *at least* 6 inches of soil depth for their roots, but if you can give them more, they'll be better off.

Common Containers and Their Volumes

Use this chart as a quick reference to find out how much soil you will need to fill standard-size containers such as clay pots, window boxes, and planters.

Basket, Hanging

10 inches	= 5.5 dry quarts	= 0.21 cu. ft.
12 inches	= 7.9 dry quarts	= 0.3 cu. ft.
14 inches	= 13.9 dry quarts	= 0.5 cu. ft.

Bowl

8 inches	= 1.9 dry quarts	= 0.07 cu. ft.
10 inches	= 3.7 dry quarts	= 0.14 cu. ft.
12 inches	= 5.5 dry quarts	= 0.21 cu. ft.
14 inches	= 8.4 dry quarts	= 0.29 cu. ft.
16 inches	= 12 dry quarts	= 0.46 cu. ft.
18 inches	= 18.8 dry quarts	= 0.73 cu. ft.
21¾ inches	= 31.2 dry quarts	= 1.21 cu. ft.

Planter, Oval

12 inches	= 3.8 dry quarts	= 0.14 cu. ft.
16 inches	= 7.3 dry quarts	= 0.28 cu. ft.
20 inches	= 9.4 dry quarts	= 0.36 cu. ft.

Planter, Square

12 inches	= 11.2 dry quarts	= 0.48 cu. ft.
15 inches	= 23 dry quarts	= 0.89 cu. ft.

Pot, Clay and Plastic

4 inches		= 1 pint
5 to 6 inches	= 1 quart	= 0.03 cu. ft.
7 to 8 inches	= 1 gallon	= 0.15 cu. ft.
8½ inches	= 2 gallons	= 0.3 cu. ft.
10 inches	= 3 gallons	= 0.46 cu. ft.
12 inches	= 5 gallons	= 0.77 cu. ft.
14 inches	= 7 gallons	= 1 cu. ft.
16 inches	= 10 gallons	= 1.5 cu. ft.
18 inches	= 15 gallons	= 2.3 cu. ft.
24 inches	= 25 gallons	= 3.8 cu. ft.
30 inches	= 30 gallons	= 4.6 cu. ft.

Pot, Strawberry

5 gallons	= 14 dry quarts	= 0.54 cu. ft.

Window Boxes

24 inches	= 11.7 dry quarts	= 0.45 cu. ft.
30 inches	= 15.6 dry quarts	= 0.6 cu. ft.
36 inches	= 19.7 dry quarts	= 0.76 cu. ft.

For larger plants such as tomatoes or potatoes, 5 gallons is a good starting point. In fact, you can even buy 5-gallon buckets from a local hardware store and grow right in those. These buckets are also wonderful for root crops such as onions, carrots, and garlic. If you want to cram more root crops in the same volume of soil, go with a shallower 5-gallon planter.

For leafy greens or other shallow-rooted plants, you can get away with a window box–style planter or any container that's at least 6 inches deep. If you want to get creative, repurpose some old boxes, jars, or containers lying around the house and start an "upcycled" garden.

The ubiquitous 5-gallon bucket makes a fantastic upcycled container garden.

The classic window planter works nicely as a kitchen herb container garden.

If you're short on space, consider odd and unique container shapes. Containers come in ovals, circles, squares, rectangles, and other interesting shapes. If you've only got a small balcony or windowsill to spare, don't despair. Grab a few square containers and line them up; they actually hold about 25 percent more soil than their circular counterparts.

One last thing to consider when it comes to volume is this: the less soil you have in your container, the more often you'll need to water. Sometimes it makes sense to use a larger container simply because the soil will stay moist longer, which means your plants' roots won't go through relentless wet-and-dry cycles, which can cause stress.

Repurposed Mason jars are a fantastic choice for the truly space-challenged urban gardener.

Growing in unique clay pots adds an aesthetic component to your container garden.

Container Materials

Choosing a material for your container is a mixture of your personal aesthetic and function. There are four major categories for materials, but don't limit yourself to these options. I've grown potatoes in sacks, tomatoes in shopping bags . . . the options are endless.

Pottery

Pottery is the classic material when you think of container gardening. Beautiful terra-cotta pots housing thriving plants is what comes to mind for most people when they think of growing in containers. While pottery is a wonderful material to use, it's important to look at the downsides of it as well.

- **Heavy**—Pottery is naturally heavy and the addition of soil only adds to the weight.
- **Porous**—Unglazed pottery will lose water to evaporation but will also protect against overwatering.
- **Brittle**—Pottery is easily shattered if it's dropped or knocked over and can crack during a freeze.

If you prefer a rustic, organic look, go with wood planter boxes or containers.

Repurposing plastic containers gives a second life to products that might otherwise end up in a landfill.

Wood

Wood is a wonderful material for container gardens. It's natural, lightweight, inexpensive, and quite durable. You can build cheap wood containers with scrap materials. It's a more popular material in raised bed gardens, so I'll dive deeper into it in that section. There are two potential downsides to growing in wood containers, however.

- **Rots**—As an organic material, wood *will* break down over time.
- **Treated**—Avoid chemically-treated wood at all costs. Wood that has been heat-treated only is okay to use.

Plastic

Plastic containers are the most plentiful and likely the cheapest ones you'll find. They're lightweight, strong, and can be molded into any shape or size you can imagine. At the same time, plastic can be incredibly damaging to our environment, and many types of plastic are unsafe to grow in.

Here are the seven different types of plastics you'll run into, and whether they're safe to grow plants.

Polyethylene Terephthalate (PET)

It's one of the most commonly recycled plastics and is almost exclusively used for single-use items such as peanut butter jars because it can break down when exposed to long periods of light or heat.

Verdict: *It's not the worst, but it's not the best. Safe to grow in for a single season; then I'd recycle.*

High-Density Polyethylene (HDPE)

You see HDPE everywhere, from milk jugs to detergent bottles. It's one of the best and safest types of plastic for food consumption because it resists UV rays and is extremely cold- and heat-tolerant (-148° to 176°F). Because of this, it's an excellent choice for the garden.

Verdict: *HDPE is one of the best types of plastic for use in the garden.*

PVC piping is handy when setting up hydroponic irrigation systems.

Not only is LDPE plastic a good option for repurposing in the garden, but you can store your harvest in it as well.

Industrial tubing made from polypropylene is a solid choice in the garden.

Polyvinyl Chloride (PVC)

One of the more commonly known types of plastic, PVC shows up in plastic pipes, irrigation, salad dressing bottles, and liquid detergent containers.

Most PVC products contain chemicals known as phthalates, which essentially help the PVC be more durable, flexible, and so forth—all of the qualities we associate with plastic. While this is great for making PVC a quality building material, phthalates are not the best for us humans. In fact, most of us have some small concentration of phthalates in our urine due to leaching, though the Centers for Disease Control (CDC) believes that our diet is the reason for most of the phthalates in our bodies.

However, not all type-3 plastics use phthalates as a plasticizer, so you may be okay using some PVC products—but make sure you know that phthalates weren't used before you make that decision.

Verdict: *PVC is okay to use as long as you don't overexpose it to light and heat or are sure that phthalate plasticizers weren't used.*

Low-Density Polyethylene (LDPE)

Some products that use LDPE include plastic produce bags, trash can liners, and food storage containers.

Are you seeing a trend here? The plastics that are already used for food storage also tend to be safe to garden with. Like its older cousin HDPE, LDPE plastic is very safe in a wide range of temperatures and can even be used in the microwave. Conclusion? It's a good choice for the garden.

Verdict: *LDPE is very safe and is not known to transmit any chemicals into soil or food. It's an excellent choice for the garden.*

Polypropylene (PP)

Polypropylene is commonly used in products that require injection molding, such as straws, bottle caps, or food containers. While it's not as universally tolerant to heat as HDPE or LDPE, it generally is safe for use with food and the garden.

There are some minor concerns about leaching that came up after Canadian researchers found that the leaching was affecting their lab work, but for the most part it's regarded as a safe plastic.

Verdict: *PP is a decent choice for the garden.*

Styrofoam cups or trays can make "okay" seed-starting containers, especially if they were otherwise going to a landfill.

Polycarbonate sheeting is fine to use to cover a greenhouse frame because it doesn't come in contact with food.

Polystyrene (PS)

You see polystyrene-based plastic everywhere, from packing peanuts, Styrofoam cups, and plastic forks to meat trays, to-go containers, and so on. It's one of the most widely used types of plastic in a variety of industries.

Being so widely used, it's also been the subject of many scientific tests on health and safety. The general conclusion is that it's safe for use in food products, which doesn't necessarily mean that it is safe for gardening. Because there are better choices, I don't use polystyrene plastics in my garden at all.

Verdict: *Seems "okay" safety-wise, but structurally PS may not be the best choice for the garden if you need it to support weight or water.*

Other Plastics

Typically, "other" means plastics made of polycarbonate or poly-lactide. Polycarbonate is the most common type-7 plastic, and also one of the most harmful plastics that we have ever created. It's been proven time and time again that it leaches BPA, which has been linked to a lot of different health problems.

Verdict: *Some type-7 plastics contain BPA, a harmful compound that has been linked to many adverse health effects. Stay away from type-7 plastics in your garden.*

Creatively repurposed metal bucket planters are lining an urban windowsill.

Felt grow bags are one of my go-to modular container gardening products.

Metal

Metal *seems* like the perfect material for a container garden: it's light, strong, and not porous like pottery. As long as the metal is properly coated (like AluZinc-coated steel), it can be an incredibly long-lasting container.

Felt Grow Bags

Over the last few years, I've become a *huge* fan of these. They come in sizes from 1 gallon all the way up to 200 gallons, which is far larger than most gardeners will ever need. They're easy to transport with their convenient handles. They don't hold too much water, as they're porous from all sides, so you won't ever rot out your plant's roots by overwatering.

If you're a renter or want to set up a container garden in the quickest possible way, give felt grow bags some serious consideration.

Old shoes and balls make for an eclectic container garden.

A tiered veggie container garden has been made from recycling old sacks.

Grab some 2-liter bottles from a neighbor and repurpose them into a beautiful hanging veggie garden.

Upcycled Containers

Don't limit yourself to buying fancy containers to get your mini garden started. There are plenty of ways to upcycle, reuse, and get creative with your container garden.

One of the simplest and most popular makeshift container gardens is growing straight in a bag of potting mix bought from a garden center. This is a great option if you're a mobility-challenged gardener, as you can plop a bag of soil on top of a table, punch some drainage holes in the bottom, cut out a section of plastic on the top, and plant away.

Let your mind go wild. Look around the house or your neighborhood for inspiration.

SACKS

The tried-and-true sack is a frugal gardener's best friend. Reusable grocery store bags, burlap bags, old coffee bags, and so on are all wonderful choices for a makeshift sack container garden. If the sacks in which you're growing are a nonporous material, just make sure to poke some drainage and aeration holes in the bottom. Avoid growing in sacks that have these characteristics:

- too thin, as they'll break under the weight of the soil
- made of an unsafe plastic
- made of paper, as they'll rot away quickly

TWO-LITER BOTTLES

Two-liter bottles are the subject of gardening experiments all over the world, and for good reason. They're plentiful, easy to work with, and would otherwise be going to a landfill. You'll see a few 2-liter bottle projects later in this book, but the sky's the limit when it comes to what you can create with these. I consider them the "Lego block" of container gardening.

Drainage holes are key when growing in containers.

Drainage

Drainage is always important when growing plants, but in container gardening it's vital that you ensure good drainage. You have to make sure that water is able to *leave* the container; otherwise, your plants' roots will drown. Remember, they need oxygen just like you and I do.

Most containers you'll pick up from a garden center already have drainage holes in the bottom, so all you'll need is a saucer to catch the water that drains out of the bottom. If you're using an unconventional container or one you've upcycled from items in your home, it's a good idea to drill a few holes in the bottom in a symmetrical pattern.

If your container bottoms don't have holes, then it's a good idea to line the container with some gravel, pebbles, or cut-up sponges to provide a little basin for extra water to settle in. However, it's doubly important not to overwater when growing in closed-bottom containers, as root rot is a major issue.

The last consideration when it comes to drainage is if you're growing in an area that you don't want water to seep out of, such as if you're growing on a balcony and you don't want the water to drip down onto unsuspecting guests below. In these cases, you can use a no-drainage container while "nesting" a smaller container within it to make sure the plant roots aren't drowning. Then, you periodically drain the larger container by hand.

Take extra care preparing and caring for your soil when growing in containers.

Filling Your Containers with Soil

I encourage you to rethink your idea of "soil" when it comes to container gardening. By their very nature, container gardens are smaller than normal gardens. They're prone to drying out, leaching nutrients, and all sorts of other issues.

Don't fret, though. Most of these problems are solved by creating perfect soil mixes for your containers.

Epic Potting Mix Recipe

This is my go-to potting mix recipe for most plants. Some plants require drastically different potting mixes, but I'll get into that later. I've provided a few modifications based on materials that are available in your region.

Of course, you can go out to a garden center and buy a high-quality potting mix as well, but it'll cost you a bit more.

If you want to DIY, here's my recipe:

- 2 parts coconut coir, peat moss, or potting soil mix (for water retention)
- 2 parts compost or composted manure (for organic matter)
- 1 part perlite or pumice (for aeration)
- ¼ to ½ part vermiculite (for water retention and aeration)

This mix is a near-perfect balance of all of the qualities that make an ideal potting mix. You'll notice I go heavier on the water retention and organic matter parts of the mix compared to a raised bed soil mix because container gardens are so prone to drying out. You should be able to find these ingredients no matter where you live, too.

MODIFICATIONS AND AMENDMENTS

An all-purpose mix is just that—best for a broad spectrum of plants. If you want to add extra ingredients to further boost your soil's fertility and quality, here are a few of my go-to picks:

- ½ to 1 part worm castings (a fantastic organic fertilizer full of nutrients)
- ½ part biochar (to improve nutrient and water retention)
- ¼ part organic fertilizer (a slow-release fertilizer that won't burn your plants)
- 2 parts perlite or pumice (for plants that need more drainage)

This south-facing balcony makes excellent use of available light.

Besides being an efficient use of space, clustering pots helps keep humidity high.

It seems that cats are genetically programmed to ruin your garden, so place your plants and containers carefully.

Where to Place Your Containers

Like most things in the garden, success often comes down to location. Make sure your containers are in a spot that will get *at least* six hours of direct sun per day for all but the most shade-tolerant veggies. If you can position them on a south-facing wall or balcony, that's even better.

Consider the wind as well. Your plants will do best in an area protected from strong gusts, which can damage foliage, dry out soil, and even knock over your containers. I've lost one too many containers to the elements, and I'll never make that mistake again . . . don't follow my lead. Use walls or windbreaks made out of fencing or fabric to protect your crops. You can also layer pots behind one another, so the larger ones protect the smaller ones.

Clustering pots together will raise the humidity in the area directly surrounding your pots, making for happier plants overall. This is an example of taking advantage of positioning to create a more favorable *microclimate* for your plants.

Finally, consider pets and children. I once received a rare fruit tree as a gift, potted it up, and proudly placed it on a balcony. I was excited to harvest my first berries, as they had the unique property of turning sour foods sweet for a period of time. Guess what happened? A cat decimated my precious tree because I didn't place it out of reach.

Not only was it a heartbreaking loss for my garden, but it could also have been dangerous for the cat if that plant had been toxic to cats. Be sure to consider other critters when it comes to container garden placement.

Which Plants Do Well in Containers?

Almost any plant can be grown in a container. The two factors to consider are the plant's root system and how big the plant gets when it's mature.

Root systems can be shallow or deep, so knowing the type your plant has helps you select the best pot for the job. For instance, growing carrots in a 6-inch-deep pot wouldn't be the best idea when most carrot varieties grow longer than over 8 inches. Similarly, growing leafy greens in 12-inch-deep containers is a bit of a waste of the container, as most leafy greens have root systems no deeper than 6 inches or so.

The size of a mature plant will also determine whether it'll survive in a container. A large indeterminate tomato plant will probably struggle without a large pot and some *serious* support, whereas a smaller variety (like the aptly named 'Patio' tomato) will not only survive but will *thrive* in a container garden environment.

Not only does it matter which plant you choose, but there are also specific varieties that work better than others due to being bred to be smaller, more compact, or more suited toward being rootbound in containers.

Here are some of my favorite plants to grow in containers, as well as the varieties that play nicely in containers.

Choosing veggie varieties suited to container growing will make all the difference.

Plant	Recommended Container	Varieties
Bean	5-gallon pot	'Dragon's Tongue', 'Blue Lake'
Beets	Wide 5-gallon pot	'Bull's Blood', 'Early Wonder'
Carrot	5-gallon pot at least 12 in. deep	'Danvers Half Long'
Cucumber	1- to 2-gallon pot	'Patio Pik'
Eggplant	5-gallon pot	'Ichiban', 'Black Beauty'
Garlic	Wide 5-gallon pot	'Music', 'French Rocambole'
Lettuce	5-gallon pot	'Merlot', 'Bibb'
Onion	Wide 5-gallon pot	'White Sweet Spanish'
Pepper	1 plant per 2-gallon pot	'Shishito', 'Purple Jalapeño'
Potatoes	5-gallon bucket	'Yukon Gold', 'Fingerling'
Radish	5-gallon pot	'Icicle', 'Cherry Belle'
Tomato	5-gallon bucket	'Early Girl', 'Patio'

A light layer of woodchip mulch protects your soil from the elements.

Keeping Your Containers Well Watered

The most common questions I get about container gardening have to do with watering. Here are some typical questions:

- How do I avoid over- or underwatering?
- Is it smart to add gravel to the bottom of my container?
- How do I keep the soil in my containers evenly moist?

It's no surprise that watering questions are common. Plants grown in containers can be prima donnas at times, demanding perfect conditions despite the cramped quarters they're living in. That said, I've collected a bunch of watering hacks over the years. Give these a try if you're struggling to keep your container garden perfectly watered.

Line Your Containers

You'll often hear to line the bottom of your containers with gravel or rocks to improve drainage. While that's an okay idea, I find that cutting up sponges and using them to line the bottom of your containers is a better option. The sponges will absorb water while still allowing excess to drain out of the holes in the bottom of your container.

Mulch Your Containers

Wait—isn't mulching reserved for raised beds or in-ground gardens? Not even close. Mulching can *drastically* reduce the amount of water your container plants need, as well as maintain stable moisture levels in your soil.

Good mulch options for containers include:

- shredded leaves
- pine needles
- bark
- gravel
- stones
- shredded newspaper

Not only will mulching prevent evaporation, but it'll also break up the water stream if you're watering with a hose or gardening can that puts out a single stream. You'll minimize soil splashing up onto the foliage, which can be a major cause of disease.

Double-Potting

As its name implies, double-potting is when you grow plants in a container that's inside a larger container. Sounds weird, right? There are a bunch of reasons you might want to use two pots per container, such as:

- You have a beautiful decorative pot that has *no drai*nage hole.
- You have interplanted two plants with different soil requirements.
- You want to keep soil moisture levels stable.

When double-potting, make sure your plant isn't sitting in water at the bottom of the larger container. You can add gravel to the bottom of the larger pot to elevate the interior pot a bit. You'll need to drain the larger pot from time to time if you have water buildup.

Use . . . Soap?

Some soil mixes, especially peat-based ones, can be hard to rehydrate if they're bone dry. If you try to water your containers and the water rolls off the soil like it's made out of concrete, then try the soap trick.

Add a drop or two of all-natural soap to your watering can and then water your garden. Soap is a *surfactant*, meaning it will lower the surface tension of water and make it easier to penetrate stubborn, dried-out soil.

Double-potting is a very simple concept: you simply place a pot inside a larger pot to create a reservoir for water.

Drip irrigation removes one of the most common problems in the garden: human error.

Automate Your Watering

If you're like me, you might forget to water your garden from time to time. You can get away with it in a raised bed, where water retention is better. But in a container garden this can spell disaster for your delicate plants. On top of that, maintaining a perfect watering schedule in the hotter months can feel like a full-time job.

The solution? Embrace your laziness and install a drip irrigation kit. When I first started container gardening, the thought of using drip irrigation sent shudders down my spine. All of the connectors, hoses, drip emitters . . . it was too much for my brain to handle.

Fortunately, it's much easier these days. You can buy simple kits that hook into a hose line, complete with all of the emitters, lines, spikes, and pressure regulators. After installing drip irrigation in my patio container garden, watering went from a twenty- to thirty-minute task once or twice a day to a one-minute task. All I do now is walk outside, turn on the nozzle, and turn it off after about half an hour.

If you want to get really fancy, add a wireless timer that you can program to automatically turn on at certain times of the day. Then you don't even have to go outside to turn on the spigot or be home at all.

Fertilizing Your Container Plants

Fertilizing your containers is *crucial* because container gardens are more prone to nutrient depletion than raised beds. This is because there's not much soil, so plants use up available nutrition quickly. Water draining out of the bottom of a container means leaching of nutrients is an issue as well.

My recommendation is to use an organic, granulated, slow-release fertilizer if possible. This will help prevent plant damage by overfertilization because, by its nature, organic fertilizer must break down before it's bioavailable for a plant's root system to absorb.

Top-dressing is the go-to method for applying organic fertilizer. Sprinkle it over the soil surface and water in well. Fertilizing with this technique is usually enough for around two to three months of growth.

If you're growing large veggies such as tomatoes and peppers, consider watering with a mixture of water and water-soluble fertilizer at about one-quarter strength dilution. The water-soluble fertilizer is available quicker and can help these heavy-feeding plants produce in small containers.

Granular organic fertilizer breaks down slowly, feeding your plants for weeks or months.

Caring for Your Container Garden

Besides all of the normal gardening tasks for growing great plants, here are a few specific to-dos to make sure your container gardens thrive.

Terra-cotta pots in particular are prone to salt buildup and a crusty appearance.

Take a little extra time and water at the base of your plants. You'll save yourself some headaches.

Clean Your Pots to Deter Diseases

On top of looking good, cleaning the outsides of your containers can help prevent diseases. Every so often, wipe them down with a wet towel or sponge to remove any clumped-up dirt.

Water Your Soil, Not Your Plants

It's a common mistake to aimlessly water over the top of your containers in the morning. When you're waking up in the morning and still rubbing the sleep out of your eyes, it's easy to grab the watering can and go to town.

Try to resist this urge. Instead, make sure to water gently right where the main stem of the plant touches the soil. Be careful not to splash soil up onto the leaves, as this is one of the main ways that soilborne pathogens and pests end up getting to your plant.

Prune the Under-Canopy

This tip doesn't apply to *all* plants, but generally speaking it's a good idea to give your plant a haircut in the area right above the soil surface. In plants with dense foliage, these leaves often aren't getting any light anyway and are not contributing much to the overall growth of the plant. Pruning them off is a great way to decrease diseases, increase airflow, and remove some of the "dead weight" your plant is carrying.

Constantly Check Soil Moisture

I hate to beat a dead horse, but soil moisture is *so* important that I'm including this tip again. Containers are an artificial environment you're creating for your plants. Keeping a close eye on your soil moisture is crucial. I recommend checking it daily when you first start container gardening. Pretty soon you'll develop a "sixth sense" about your containers and won't have to be *as* diligent . . . but it takes time, so be patient.

Getting rid of undergrowth helps increase airflow and prevent soilborne diseases from making their way to your plants.

Check soil moisture daily until you develop an understanding of how much water your container plants need.

Most of the materials you'll need for this project are already lying around your house.

Sub-Irrigated Two-Liter Bottle Gardens

Also known as self-watering containers, a sub-irrigated container is one that waters your plants from the bottom via wicking action. You'll use a wicking material to pull water from the bottom of the container into the soil, where it will be sucked up by the plant's root zone and used. These systems are incredibly water-conscious, often needing watering two to three times less often than a normal container garden. On top of that, they save you time and ensure your soil is evenly moist 24/7.

Materials

- 2-liter bottle
- scissors
- felt strips or an old cotton T-shirt
- potting mix
- seeds or seedlings
- wrapping material (optional)

Steps

1. Remove the label from your 2-liter bottle, taking care to remove as much of the sticky part as possible. Take scissors and poke drainage holes on the curved top section of the bottle. These holes will ensure the soil doesn't get *too* wet once we plant our seedlings.

2. Using your scissors, puncture the bottle 1 inch below where it stops curving, then cut horizontally across in a straight line until the bottle is in two pieces.

3. Fill the bottle with water until it reaches the bottom of the soil basin. Flip the top piece of the bottle into the bottom piece. Take your felt strip or old piece of T-shirt and thread it through the bottle top, making sure it reaches the bottom of the bottle but still extends 2 to 3 inches into the soil basin.

4. Fill with soil and add your plants. If soil is spilling through to the reservoir, add a couple of rocks to the bottom.

Optional: If you want extra style points, use wrapping paper to hide the bottle. Not only does this look nice, but it also blocks light from reaching the water, preventing algae buildup. *Voilà*—you now have a low-maintenance herb and greens garden that can be replicated as many times as you want, placed wherever you want, and enjoyed.

Caring for Your Self-Watering Bottle

As the name implies, you don't have to do too much to take care of this container. Keep an eye on the water level and simply lift the basin out and refill it when it runs low. Depending on what you grow, you'll want to add a little granulated organic fertilizer after about a month of growth to make sure the soil still has the nutrition it needs to keep your plants thriving.

Step 2

Make sure to cut below the curved section; otherwise, the top will drop into the bottle.

Step 3

Make sure your cloth extends into the soil basin; otherwise, your plant's roots won't get water.

Step 4

A finished 2-liter garden has been planted with lemon balm, ready to grow on autopilot.

As with most of these projects, scrounging around the house and a quick trip to the hardware store is likely all you'll need to do to collect your materials.

Self-Watering 5-Gallon Bucket

Containers come in all shapes and sizes, but one of the most plentiful is the classic 5-gallon bucket. Found at big-box stores around the world, these can easily be modified for a variety of different container gardening designs.

This project turns your 5-gallon bucket into a self-watering garden, perfect for herbs, greens, beans, tomatoes, or peppers. When buying a bucket, keep in mind that dark colors absorb heat and light colors reflect heat. Where you place your self-watering container garden will determine the color you should choose.

Materials

- 5-gallon bucket with lid
- drill
- 1-inch paddle bit
- X-acto knife
- 5-inch wood or plastic spacers
- old cotton T-shirt
- 1-inch PVC pipe
- ¼-inch drill bit
- potting soil
- plants
- piece of foam (optional)

Steps

1. Secure the lid to the top of the bucket and drill two 1-inch holes, one in the middle of the lid and one offset 1 inch from the edge.

2. With an X-acto knife, carefully cut out the interior of the lid, taking care not to cut into the offset hole you drilled.

3. Place your spacers in the bottom of the bucket and drape an old cotton T-shirt into the bucket.

4. Fit the PVC pipe through the offset hole and lower the lid into the bottom of the bucket, pressing it firmly against the spacers. Wrap the T-shirt around the top of the lid, and stuff the excess fabric into the hole in the center of the lid.

5. Drill two drainage holes with the ¼-inch bit in the side of the bucket about ½ inch below where the lid sits. These holes prevent you from overfilling the bucket with water.

6. Fill the bucket with soil and transplant your plants, then fill the PVC pipe with water until water starts to run out of the drainage holes at the bottom of the bucket. Snap the outside edge of the lid back on top of the bucket.

Optional: If you want an easy water level indicator, cut a thin strip of foam and drop it into the PVC pipe as your water line measurer. It will slowly drop as your plant uses up the water in the sub-irrigated section.

Step 1

The center hole is for wicking and the offset hole is for your water line measurer.

Step 2

Cut a circle around the inside of the lid, leaving 1 inch of lid for later.

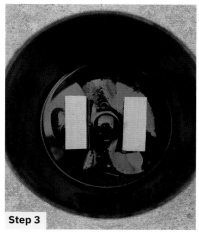

Step 3

The spacers ensure your lid doesn't sink into the water reservoir.

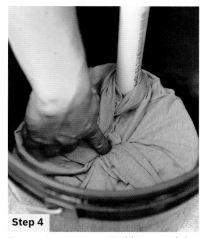

Step 4

Be sure to wrap your T-shirt around the lid; otherwise, it won't wick well.

Step 5

These drainage holes ensure you'll never waterlog your bucket and rot your plant's roots.

Step 6

Use a 1-inch PVC pipe with some foam as a water level indicator and potential trellis.

Caring for Your Self-Watering Bucket

As long as you remember to refill the chamber with water, your plants will grow vigorously in this system. Be sure to fertilize with organic granulated fertilizer from time to time and use supports if you're growing a climbing plant or one that puts on heavy fruits, such as tomatoes.

If you want to protect the soil surface, you can either mulch or you can cut a circle of landscape fabric with a hole in the middle for your plant's stem to fit through. Then place it on top of the bucket and snap the outer ring of the lid back on to keep it nice and tight.

I used milk crates for this project, but any upcycled container will do.

Upcycled Container Garden

You don't need to spend a pretty penny at the local nursery or big-box store to have a thriving, beautiful container garden. Oftentimes you can arrange gorgeous and functional gardens out of stuff you've got lying around the house.

I also recommend asking local groceries or recycling centers for old containers; you'd be surprised what they're willing to part with. I've gotten milk crates, pallets, and other plastic containers for free, simply by asking.

Step 2

Placing landscape fabric around the sides of porous containers will prevent soil, water, and nutrient leakage.

Materials

- milk crates, grocery boxes, or some other upcycled container
- drill and ¼-inch drill bit (optional)
- landscape fabric liner (optional)
- potting soil
- plants

Steps

1. Take stock of the containers you've collected. If you're going to grow in plastic containers, be sure to look at the bottom of the container to determine the type of plastic. Refer to the materials section earlier in this chapter to see if it's safe to grow in.

2. Drill drainage holes into any makeshift containers that don't have them. Consider adding landscape fabric liner on some of the more porous containers, like milk crates.

3. After you've prepared your containers, the rest of the planting process is the same as any other container garden . . . except you get to customize the look to your exact desires. Stacking, layering, and clustering are all fantastic design techniques not only from an aesthetic perspective, but also as space savers.

4. When planting and placing your containers, think about how your plants will grow. For instance, placing a tomato plant front and center might not be the best idea due to its size and need to grow vertically. Instead, place that in the back of your container garden and put shorter, stubbier plants such as leaf lettuce and herbs front and center.

The beauty of upcycled containers is their ability to make use of otherwise wasted growing space.

3

Raised Bed Gardening

Raised beds are one of the most popular urban gardening methods, understandably so. There are a million and one good reasons to grow in raised beds as opposed to in-ground, *especially* in urban environments. Plus, they *look beautiful,* no matter what style of raised bed you decide to build.

That said, many gardeners get overwhelmed when thinking about starting their own raised beds with questions such as:

- **What materials should I use?**
- **How do I harvest successive crops, week after week?**
- **How do I maintain my beds, year after year?**

Answers to all of these questions, along with step-by-step plans, await you in this chapter.

Repurposed pallet collars growing an abundance of rhubarb.

The Many Advantages of Raised Beds

For an urban gardener, the first and most important advantage to growing in raised beds is space and customization. If you don't have any soil to grow plants in-ground, a raised bed may be your only option. On top of that, you can build them to any size and shape, fill with soil, and begin planting. This makes them extremely flexible for the space-conscious gardener.

Better Soil

Along with space efficiency comes improved soil. Unless you have naturally fertile soil on your property, chances are the soil you mix for your raised bed will be a more complete source of nutrients for your plants. It'll also have the right texture, ample drainage, and be easier to work.

Better Drainage

Even if your in-ground soil is fertile, many first-time gardeners have a hard time with compaction and drainage. Raised beds solve this problem in two ways: first, they're raised up off the ground, which gives water some room to drain down; second, you're mixing your own soil and can adjust the mix to alter how much water your soil holds.

Increased Yield

Raised beds *typically* increase the yield per plant as well. You can start your plants earlier in the season because raised bed soil warms up earlier. Second, you're able to use space more effectively and plant more densely.

Less Weeding

Most raised beds block annoying weeds from coming up from the ground, especially if you line the bottom with weed cloth or landscape fabric.

Easy to Grow In

Finally, an often overlooked benefit of growing in a raised bed is how *easy* they are to work in. You can raise them as high as you like, even opting for standing raised beds if you have a hard time bending over.

All of these benefits make them one of the most flexible gardening methods available to you, so let's learn how to grow in them.

A Square Foot Garden is a classic system that takes advantage of all of the pluses of growing in raised beds.

Mounded beds with wooden planks as pathways is about as simple as a raised bed garden gets.

Raised Bed Materials

Like container gardening, you have a lot of flexibility when it comes to what materials to use. The simplest is to use no materials at all. You can mound soil up in a row around 2 to 4 feet wide. Of course, you'll lose some of the advantages we talked about, but if you're low on budget or materials, the "no edges" raised bed will work just fine.

If you want your beds to be more permanent, consider building from wood, concrete blocks, bricks, or metal.

Wood

The classic material to build your beds is wood. You can use boards, 4×4s, railroad ties—anything you can get your hands on. If you can buy cedar, your beds will last much longer, as cedar rots very slowly compared to other woods.

If you're using boards from a hardware store, try using L-shaped brackets to attach the boards together. They're much stronger and more stable than nailing boards together. Better yet, use posts driven into the ground and attach your boards to the posts. The options here really are endless, as long as you make sure you construct something sturdy.

WHAT TYPE OF WOOD IS SAFE FOR GARDENING?

There's a lot of debate about the right type of wood to use in the garden. The two best types of wood are untreated cedar and redwood, but both of these can be hard to find and pricey. Your next best bets are hemlock, fir, or pine, but they don't last as long. Still, they're more accessible and cheaper, meaning replacing them will cost you less over the years.

PRESSURE-TREATED WOOD: GOOD OR BAD?

If you want to use pressure-treated wood, I wouldn't recommend it. It's been controversial for years now due to the chemicals used in the pressure-treating process. It lasts much longer than untreated wood but at the risk of potentially leaching chemicals into the garden.

No matter what, avoid chromated copper arsenate (CCA)–treated wood (removed from the market nearly twenty years ago), as it's the most controversial treatment. A more recent treatment like alkaline copper quaternary (ACQ) is a lower risk according to the Environmental Protection Agency (EPA), but is still riskier than using untreated wood.

My personal decision is to construct my wood beds from untreated Douglas fir whenever I have the option; I like the combination of looks, price, and safety.

Concrete

Concrete building blocks are a wonderful, stable, and cheap building material for beds. You don't even need to add mortar unless you're building more than three blocks high. Each block should overlap one-half of each block below it.

Brick

Bricks are an amazing building material if you can get your hands on some. They also add a nice contrast between your soil and your beds if you care about the aesthetics of your beds. The only downside is that they're brittle and prone to breaking or chipping over time. If you're building a large raised bed, you'll want to make sure they're supported as well.

Metal or Prefabricated

Most metal raised beds are sold as raised bed garden kits. There's *nothing* wrong with grabbing a kit if you don't have the materials or the desire to build your own. They're

Wooden raised beds can be as simple or as fancy as your heart (or budget) desires.

Corrugated, Aluzinc-coated metal beds from Birdie's Garden Products is my go-to raised bed these days.

often lightweight and gorgeous, adding some real sparkle to the garden. The only things to consider with a metal bed is if they've been coated properly to avoid leaching, and if they are painted a lighter color on the outside to avoid heat retention.

Lining the bottom of your beds with landscape fabric prevents all but the most ambitious weeds from growing.

Constructing the Bed

A good rule of thumb on sizing raised beds is to build beds no wider than 4 feet on any side. This is because your arm only has about a 2-foot reach, so a 4-foot bed is easily accessible from any side at any time.

If you're setting up more than one raised bed, be careful to leave enough room between beds. The last thing you want to do is squeeze them so closely together that you can't work in between beds. I recommend 20 to 24 inches between beds as a minimum. This allows you to get in there and prune, harvest, or water without any issues.

Lining Your Beds

You have a few options for lining the bottom of your beds. The method you choose depends on the problem that you most anticipate having.

If your space is prone to gnarly weeds, then laying down a heavy landscape fabric will suffocate them while still allowing enough air and water through without affecting the drainage of your bed.

If you'd rather not use any plastic, laying down old newspaper and topping off with old cardboard will do a good job too. However, after enough time, cardboard will rot and weeds may start penetrating your bed.

If you struggle more with burrowing pests than weeds, consider hardware cloth instead. It's deceptively named, as it's actually a heavy-duty wire mesh and not a fabric. As you might imagine, it's impossible for larger pests to burrow through this mesh, but weeds have an easy time penetrating the large holes.

The ultimate solution is to line the bottom with *both*, but this usually isn't necessary. It's just the safest option if you want no problems at all in your bed.

Hardware "cloth" is a misnomer for this ¼-inch metal wire mesh that prevents all burrowing pests from penetrating it.

Raised Bed Placement

Just like real estate, bed placement is all about location, location, location. If you want epic harvests, you'll want to locate your raised bed facing south. This is the direction that gets the most sun exposure over the course of the day if you're in the Northern Hemisphere. If you can't, then a southwestern- or southeastern-facing site is your next best bet.

Consider how windy the area gets, as well as if there are any features such as trees, bushes, or buildings that are going to block the sun for a period of the day. I highly recommend observing a few potential locations over the course of a day and monitoring how shadows are thrown across the space.

To understand how the sun will fall on your property throughout the year, check out the tool www.suncalc.net.

Filling Your Beds with Soil

Now that your beds are built and placed in an amazing growing location, it's time to fill them up with life-giving soil. You need to consider two things: how much soil you need and how to create an amazing soil mix.

CALCULATING SOIL NEEDS

The absolute minimum soil depth you can get away with is 4 inches, but I highly recommend going at least 6 to 12 inches deep with your soil. The deeper the better, especially if you are growing veggies such as carrots, leeks, or any deep-rooted plant.

Figuring out how much total soil you need is a simple math equation:

Length × Width × Height = Soil Volume

If you have a 4-foot × 4-foot × 1-foot bed, for example, you've got 16 cubic feet of space to fill with soil. Adjust these figures to the size of your bed and you're off to the next step, which is how to mix your soil.

CREATING THE PERFECT SOIL MIX

From the "Soil, the Bedrock of Your Garden" section of this book on page 34, you know that good soil needs a balance of organic matter, water retention, and aeration.

For organic matter, compost is your best bet. You can buy quality bags of organic compost from a garden center or see if your city has a composting program and will give you some for free. Free is always better, as long as it's not full of nasty stuff. Get compost from as many different sources as possible for a more complete nutrient profile.

For water retention, you can use either peat moss or coconut coir. These days, I prefer coconut coir, which is made of shredded coconut husks. It's more sustainable than peat moss and soaks up water like a dry sponge, whereas peat moss can be harder to rehydrate if it's bone dry. You can buy coconut coir as dehydrated bricks, making them extremely cheap to ship as well.

For aeration, you need something to "fluff up" your soil. Good options here are perlite, vermiculite, and pumice, in that order.

Mix it all together, add a dash of your favorite soil amendment (I like worm castings), and you're off to the races.

Hundreds of leafy greens seedlings are getting ready for their life in raised beds.

Planting Your Beds

Finally. It's time to get your beds planted. The first question to answer here is whether you should start plants from seed or buy transplants and plop them into the soil. Both methods are viable, but one requires a bit more knowledge than the other.

Seeds vs. Transplants

There's no better feeling in the world than eating a veggie you grew all the way from seed to harvest. Growing from seed is cheaper, as you can get a packet of hundreds of seeds for the same cost as three to six transplants. However, there's no such thing as a free lunch. By growing from seed, you're paying in *time* what transplants cost in *money*.

If you're a beginner gardener, I'd recommend skipping out on starting from seed and opting for the transplant route. You'll pay a bit more, but you're buying weeks or even months of plant development for your money. You also skip out on the many problems you can run into when starting plants from seed. However, if you're really set in starting plants from seed, check out "An Age-Old Debate: Seeds vs. Transplants" on page 50 for complete instructions.

How to Space Seedlings in Your Beds

Almost anything you can grow in the ground can be grown in a raised bed as long as you give it ample space. There are a million and one different spacing systems you can follow, but all of them use a few basic principles. Understand these, and you'll know exactly how to space all of your plants for the rest of your life.

In urban environments, high-density plant spacing is your best friend. Unlike row planting, high-density planting seeks to cram as many plants as possible into a bed. Traditional row planting is usually designed for industrial-size farming or market gardening, where you must have large spaces between plants for gas- or hand-powered tools.

In the home garden, you'll be doing most of the work by hand, so high-density planting is the way to go. The increased shade caused by tightly spaced plants has many benefits, such as:

- water loss is minimized
- soil is protected from the sun's rays
- weeds can't get enough light to thrive

Here's a spacing cheat sheet for some of the most common raised bed veggies.

Buying transplants avoids common seed-starting mistakes that can stop your garden dead in its tracks.

Vegetable	Inches	Vegetable	Inches
Asparagus	15–18	Lettuce, head	10–12
Bean, bush	4–6	Lettuce, leaf	4–6
Bean, lima	4–6	Melon	18–24
Bean, pole	6–12	Mustard	6–9
Beet	2–4	Okra	12–18
Broccoli	12–18	Onion	2–4
Brussels sprouts	15–18	Peas	2–4
Cabbage	15–18	Peppers	12–15
Cabbage, Chinese	10–12	Potato	10–12
Carrot	2–3	Pumpkin	24–36
Cauliflower	15–18	Radish	2–3
Chard, Swiss	6–9	Rutabaga	4–6
Collards	12–15	Southern pea	3–4
Cucumber	12–18	Spinach	4–6
Eggplant	18–24	Squash, summer	18–24
Endive	15–18	Squash, winter	24–36
Kale	15–18	Sweet corn	15–18
Kohlrabi	6–9	Tomato	18–24
Leeks	3–6	Turnip	4–6

Protecting Your Precious Plants

The beauty of raised bed gardening is how easy it is to attach extra equipment to your beds to provide protection from the weather and extend the growing season. Let's go over a few methods for both.

Protect fragile seedlings from birds and the elements with a repurposed plastic bottle.

You can drastically extend your growing season with a simple cold frame design.

Plastic Bottles

Plastic bottles can act as a "mini-greenhouse" for fragile transplants, seedlings, or cuttings. Slice a bottle in half and place it over the top of your seedling, then press the edges into the soil. To ensure airflow, you can drill a few holes into the bottle and remove the cap from the top half. This is also a great way to protect young seedlings from inquisitive birds or early pests, which often like to munch on tender young upstarts.

Cold Frames

Cold frames are just what they sound like—an incredible way to protect crops from a cold snap. They let sunlight in, so your plants keep growing as well as warm up the interior air. Most cold frame designs can be done on the cheap using old windows, doors, and other upcycled parts.

Cold frames typically aren't heated because they rely on the sun's energy and the greenhouse effect to keep the interior nice and toasty. However, you'll need to insulate them well if you want the heating effect to be significant. Make sure you have a tight seal on your cold frame.

Polytunnels

Polytunnels, also known as hoop houses, are one of the most accessible ways to protect your crops from the elements and extend the season. At their most basic, they're constructed of hoops, bars, and a cover of polyethlene plastic. With this simple contraption, you can start your season earlier and grow your plants well after frost.

Greenhouses

Greenhouses are a fantastic way to bookend the growing season, allowing you to start seeds earlier and grow crops later into the fall and winter.

They don't need to be as fancy as the ones you see on the right, either. You can buy or make simple, small greenhouses with enough space to give your seed starting a head start in the spring.

Polytunnels can be purchased, but they're easy to string together with a few store-bought materials too.

A quality greenhouse can drastically extend your growing season.

Carrots planted in succession show three different stages of growth.

Method One: Plant Different Varieties of the Same Plant

The easiest way to get continual harvests is to plant different varieties of the same plant that come to maturity at different dates. For example, you could plant these three varieties of tomatoes at *exactly the same time*, but harvest tomatoes for months due to the difference in their days to maturity:

- 'Early Girl' – 54 days
- 'Champion' – 65 days
- 'Golden Boy' – 80 days

By planting these three varieties, you'll have a solid month of guaranteed tomatoes, plus at least another two to four weeks of continual harvesting from the same plants. That brings it to a total of two months of successive tomato harvests.

How to Harvest Week After Week

One of the most common questions I get is, "Kevin, how do I plant so I get a consistent harvest week after week?" It's a *great* question, and one that is extremely confusing when you start gardening.

First, let's introduce the concept of *succession planting,* or timing your plantings so you get multiple harvests of the same crop over the course of a season. Every time you harvest one crop, you plant another in its place and repeat the process.

Method Two: Start New Seeds on a Schedule

Another approach to succession planting is to continually *start* new plants as you harvest old ones. This method works well for plants that are easy to start from seed and transplant well. This is also where most gardeners get a bit confused, because you have to work *backward from the end of your season* rather than forward. We're not used to thinking that way.

To illustrate this principle, imagine you have a three-month (ninety-day) growing season and you're growing radishes, which take about thirty days to mature. If you just planted a new crop of radishes after harvesting the old ones, you could only get three crops of radishes in . . . which might not be what you want. If you want radishes every week, how do you get them?

The answer is to start new radish seeds every seven days, and you'll be able to harvest radishes once a week.

Here's how it looks:

- **Week 1:** 1 batch of radishes planted
- **Week 2:** 1 batch planted, 1 batch at 1 week old
- **Week 3:** 1 batch planted, 1 batch each at 1 and 2 weeks old
- **Week 4:** 1 batch planted, 1 batch each at 1, 2, and 3 weeks old
- **Week 5:** 1 batch harvested, 1 batch planted, and 1 batch each at 1, 2, and 3 weeks old

While this doesn't change the *amount* of radishes you'll harvest (assuming you're growing in the same space), it evens out the harvests so you have a more consistent supply of fresh produce for your meals.

Succession Planting Quick Reference Chart	
Crop	**Planting Interval (days)**
Radish	7
Spinach	7
Head lettuce	10
Asian greens	10
Peas	10
Sweet corn	10
Bush bean	10
Beet	14
Endive	14
Arugula	14
Turnip	14
Carrot	21
Cucumber	21
Melon	21
Summer squash	30
Swiss chard	30

You can keep this schedule going as long as your growing season allows. Instead of harvesting radishes only three times in your season, you're harvesting them twelve times per season.

I recommend only succession planting crops that you *absolutely love* and use on a regular basis, as it can get complex to track multiple plantings of multiple crops. I personally succession plant carrots, leafy greens, and beans.

Wood chip mulch is an incredible way to build soil over the winter.

Maintaining Your Beds Year After Year

Of all of the urban gardening methods in this book, raised beds are by far the most permanent. While you don't *have* to, you might want to grow in your beds year after year. Here are some of my top tips for keeping your beds productive every single year.

Clean Your Beds in the Fall

Once fall approaches, it's time to shut your raised beds down. Unless you're growing under cover or live in a warm climate, this is the time to do a bit of garden cleanup. Many gardeners think it's a good idea to scoop up all of the debris from the garden—but nothing could be further from the truth.

Beneficial insects, microbes, and fungi all enjoy your garden debris over late fall to winter. It provides them with cover, warmth, and food. Better yet, once spring rolls around, the ecosystem in your garden will be more resilient than ever.

Of course, if you have diseased plants or an overwhelming amount of debris, you can definitely get rid of some of it. But as a general rule, try not to sweep everything away from your fall beds.

Amend Your Soil Before Winter

If you harvest from your beds season after season without doing anything to replace the nutrients that you've taken from the soil, your beds will suffer. It's time to improve your soil.

Add 1 to 2 inches of compost, well-rotted manure, or your favorite organic amendment. You don't need to get crazy here—adding directly to the top of your beds and spreading evenly is completely fine. Over the winter, the nutrients within will break down and, come spring, they'll be ready for your plants to enjoy.

If, like me, you live in a warm climate and can grow year-round, then you'll need to amend your beds twice a year: once at the end of the warm season and once at the end of the cool season.

Don't Forget to Mulch

For some reason, gardeners often neglect mulching their beds. I'm not sure why this happens, because the benefits of mulching are *immense,* including these:

- less weed pressure
- retains moisture in soil
- keeps soil cool
- improves soil life

You don't need anything fancy here. Grass clippings, chopped leaves, or wood chips make perfectly good mulches. Add no more than 1 to 2 inches of mulch to the top of your beds after you amend them, and your beds will thank you for it.

Regardless of what type of gardening you do, the fall is a good time to add amendments to your soil, especially if you grow organically. Organic fertilizer releases more slowly and overwintering it gives you a head start.

Rotate Your Plantings

Even if you amend and mulch your beds, it's still a good idea to switch up what you plant in each bed every so often. Heavy-feeders such as tomatoes, squash, and cucumbers should be rotated every season to ensure you're not depleting one section of your garden more than others. On top of that, many pests and plant diseases prefer certain plants, so switching up where they're located in the garden season after season is a great way to reduce their prevalence.

Dead-Simple Raised Bed

It doesn't get easier than this . . . a simple raised bed design made with eight total items using *no nails, screws, or power tools*. It's perfect for you if you have these restrictions:

- rent your living space and don't want to build a permanent raised bed
- aren't too handy and want something simple to build
- don't have a lot of money to invest in your garden at the moment

The design relies on the use of planter wall blocks, which are concrete-molded and slotted to fit 2 × 6-inch pieces of lumber. You'll need at least four of these as well as some 2 × 6-inch lumber of your choosing.

Materials
- 2 × 6-inch lumber, cut to size
- 4 planter wall blocks
- 2 × 4-inch lumber, cut to size (optional)
- drill and screws (optional)
- soil mix
- plants

Steps
1. For easy assembly, get your lumber cut to size when you buy it. As far as dimensions go, fit this garden to your unique growing environment. If you need a few suggestions for classic sizes, you can't go wrong with any of these:
- 4 × 4-feet
- 2 × 4-feet
- 4 × 8-feet

2. After your lumber is cut, clear and level the ground on which you're going to place the planter wall blocks. This is key, as this is a slide-in assembly raised bed. Once your ground is level, simply slide your 2 × 6-inch boards into the slots in the planter wall blocks and you're done with the main construction.

3. If you want to add a layer of weed or pest protection, line the bottom of your newly-constructed bed with landscape fabric or hardware cloth. You can also lay down a few sheets of cardboard for a lining that will break down over time and build your soil while smothering weeds in the short term.

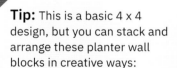

Tip: This is a basic 4 x 4 design, but you can stack and arrange these planter wall blocks in creative ways:
- Stack multiple planter blocks on top of one another to create a taller raised bed.
- Screw 2 × 4-inch boards to the top of your beds as ledges for seating while you garden.
- Create odd-shaped designs to fit unique spaces in your gardening area.

Step 1

If you're a total beginner to raised beds, this plan is my go-to recommendation.

Step 2

The planter blocks are designed to perfectly fit a 2 × 6-inch piece of lumber in their slots.

Step 3

Line the bottom with landscape fabric or hardware cloth if you have weed or pest issues.

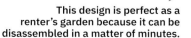

▶

This design is perfect as a renter's garden because it can be disassembled in a matter of minutes.

Herbs and small leafy greens work well inside the holes of each block.

Masonry Raised Bed

If you don't want to build your beds from wood, a masonry garden is a great option. By combining chimney tiles with cement blocks, you can build a bed that's not only customized to the size you want but also comes with built-in posts and ledges either to sit on or plant into.

Masonry gardens are great if you're not too handy or are gardening on a property you rent, because you don't want to construct permanent raised beds.

You can often find discarded masonry on Craigslist or around the neighborhood.

2. Before you lay out your block pattern, decide if you want to lay down hardware cloth, landscape fabric, old newspaper, or another type of barrier. I recommend hardware cloth for pest-prone gardens and landscape fabric for weed-prone gardens. If you have both problems, then use both.

3. Start in one corner of your garden, laying down a chimney block. Then lay your cinder blocks out and finish the pattern. It's that simple—the construction of this bed is *done*.

4. Fill with your raised bed soil mix and start planting. You can leave the holes in the chimney and cinder blocks empty or fill them with soil and plant into them. I like to plant the chimney blocks with pollinator-attracting flowers and dedicate the rest of the bed space to edibles. It's a great way to get bees and other pollinators doing some work for you in the garden.

Materials
- landscape fabric (optional)
- 4 or more chimney blocks
- 4 or more cinder blocks (you need at least 4, but you can add more to your desired bed size)
- soil mix
- plants

Steps
1. As with any construction project, make sure you select the right site and level the ground. You're lining blocks up, so unless you don't mind a messy top edge, it's important to get the ground nice and level. You can even sink the blocks partially into the ground if you want extra stability in your design.

Classic Raised Bed

It doesn't get easier than this . . . a simple raised bed design made with the most basic cuts of wood. These materials should be accessible no matter where you live. In fact, you might have some old pieces lying around the house that you can repurpose into this raised bed design.

Materials for this bed design often cost under $20, making it an affordable option.

Materials

- 4 cedar fence panels, ½ inch × 5½ inches × 4 feet
- 1 baluster, 2 × 2 × 36 inches
- circular saw
- drill and driver bits
- square
- 16 deck screws, ½ inch
- landscape fabric

Steps

1. This design is for a classic 4-foot × 4-foot garden with 4-inch balusters in the corners, perfectly accessible from any side, but feel free to modify it to your own specifications. Cut your fence panels and baluster to size with a circular saw (or ask the lumberyard to do it for you).

2. Pre-drill your holes in each piece of wood so they don't crack, especially due to the thin siding used for this project.

3. Working on a flat surface, line your corners up and use a square to ensure they're perfectly aligned. The last thing you want is a crooked bed. Sink your deck screws into each corner to create the initial frame for the bed.

4. Add the baluster pieces to each corner, and screw those in for additional support. Make sure to screw two screws into each side of each corner for increased stability.

5. You can add hardware cloth to the bottom if you have problems with burrowing pests, landscape fabric if you have weed issues, or support posts in the middle of each board to prevent bowing if you design extremely long beds.

6. Now you should have a 4-foot × 4-foot × 5½-inch-tall raised bed that's super sturdy and ready for planting.

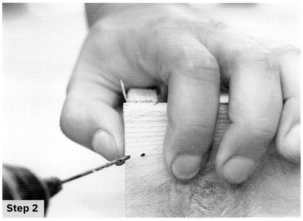

Step 2

When building with thin wood, pilot holes are absolutely necessary.

Step 3

Make sure the surface is level and square as you sink your deck screws into the fence panels.

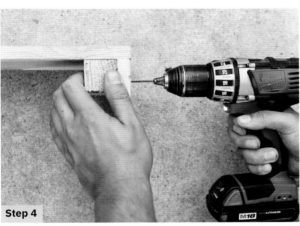

Step 4

The baluster adds extra rigidity so your beds won't warp and bend out of shape once you add soil.

Step 5

Landscape fabric is recommended to help keep down weeds or grass growing from your native soil.

Step 6

Fill the bed with soil, transplant, water in, and get growing.

4

Vertical Gardening

For the space-challenged gardener, there's no better method to learn than vertical gardening. Instead of treating the ground under your feet as the only growing space you have, consider the fact that there's an entire world *above* the ground to take advantage of.

Besides the space savings, the advantages of vertical gardening are almost endless, including:

- **less weeding and maintenance**
- **fewer diseases and pests due to better air circulation**
- **easy access is better for less wear and tear on your body**
- **perfect for growing vining-type plants in minimal space**

Where to Build Your Vertical Garden

The beauty of vertical gardening is the fact that you need far less space than many other growing methods. You can get away with a growing space about 1 to 2 feet wide and 6 inches deep, because you're growing *up, not out.* With these benefits come unique considerations as far as where to locate a vertical garden.

The first is whether you're going to build supports for a freestanding vertical garden or if you're going to build it next to an existing structure such as a fence or wall. If you're growing against a wall, avoid a north-facing one because you'll get almost no sunlight over the course of a day. If you only have a north-facing wall, then choose shade-tolerant plants such as spinach, lettuce, and other greens. The perfect location is south-facing, as that gets the highest amount of direct sunlight over a day.

If you're building a freestanding vertical garden, then you need to consider sunlight, wind, and support structures. The increased amount of sunlight your garden will get due to growing upward will actually steal light from anything you grow below it, so take care not to grow sun-loving plants in the shadows of your vertical garden. If you're growing vertically on a balcony or other windy area, you need to take extra care to secure your supports to the ground or risk losing your garden to the elements.

A simple trellis tacked onto a common planter box extends the growing capabilities significantly.

Morning glories are shown twining around a wood-and-bamboo fence.

The tendrils of a young pumpkin plant have attached themselves to a coconut coir rope.

Twining Vines

With twining vines, the lead shoots of plants such as morning glories will twirl around supports as they climb. They cast a wide arc until they find something to latch on to. When supporting vines like this, you can get away with anything that allows them to wrap fully around.

Tendrils

Plants that climb with tendrils are a different beast. Instead of a plant twirling its lead shoot around a support, they have antennae-like structures that flail about until they find a support. Then they wind themselves tightly around that. Peas are one of the most iconic tendril-climbing plants you'll grow in your veggie garden.

If your tendril-climbing plants don't find supports quickly, they may collapse and start to twirl around themselves. Their "antennae" will hit the plant itself, think it's a support, and create a tangled mess. Chicken-wire fences and trellis netting are wonderful ways to control these climbers (compared to bamboo stakes).

How Plants Climb

The support you choose for any climbing plant is in part determined by how that plant climbs upward. Nature designed a few different ingenious methods for plants to naturally climb structures.

Vining plants love to grow fast, but that fast growth often comes at a tradeoff of not being able to support their own weight. Their root systems are typically extensive, giving them the energy to produce vigorous vertical growth.

It's your job to be a helping hand and give them something to hang on to as they make their journey upward. Keep in mind, some of these plants are so vigorous that they don't want to *stop* climbing . . . so be sure to prune them.

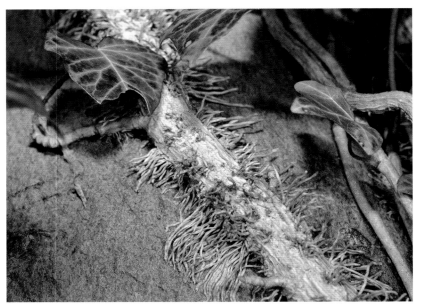
The aerial root structure of invasive English ivy is tenacious.

Aerial Roots

Aerial roots are the easiest climbing plants to grow. In fact, they're almost *too easy*, as evidenced by the main plant in this category: English ivy. Ivy is an invasive plant in many areas, mostly due to its vigorous growth and its ability to climb with aerial roots. They grow from a plant's stem and quickly adhere to anything they touch. They're so aggressive that they can even rip paint off of walls if you let them get too crazy.

Thorns

Some plants prefer a more rugged approach, growing thorns and using them to stick themselves to structures for their support. For example, thorny blackberries can easily climb up a trellis, as long as you gently guide them through the trellis as they grow.

Roses are the classic example of a thorny climbing plant.

This cucumber plant's tendrils didn't attach to the trellis, so a twisttie has been used to provide support.

Supporting Plants That Don't Support Themselves

If you want to grow plants that nature didn't bless with a built-in climbing method, it's time to employ the power of technology. Here are a few ideas for ways to secure plants to your trellis or vertical garden structure:

- **Zip ties**—These are cheap and easy. Zip these around stems but keep them loose to allow further thickening of the stem.
- **Twist ties**—Upcycle these from the grocery store, but don't tie too tightly; the thin metal wire can slice right through sensitive plant matter.

- **Twine**—This is great to run between support structures and provide something for a plant to grow horizontally across. Twine can also be dropped down vertically to allow plants to climb up it directly.
- **Tape**—If it's all you've got, tape works well. Wrap some tape around vulnerable stems.
- **Trellis clips**—Buy trellis clips at any local nursery or online. They're fantastic for quickly snapping on to support plants that set a lot of fruit, like tomatoes, cucumbers, and so on, and they're reusable, so they're a great investment.

- **Nylons/tights**—It might sound silly, but nylons are an amazing way to support large fruits on vining plants, such as melons. You can use them as a sling to take some of the weight off of the vine.

The Many Ways to Grow Vertically

The beauty of vertical gardening is the raw creativity you can employ. If you can imagine it, you can build it in a vertical system. Here are some of my favorite ways to grow vertically with creative materials.

This wood-and-string trellis makes excellent use of the vining nature of tomatoes.

Trellises

Trellises are the go-to when it comes to vertical gardening. They come in all shapes and sizes, especially if you opt to DIY. If you want the fastest and easiest trellis possible, hit a big-box store and pick one up. However, they'll be pricier than you might want to pay, as well as constructed out of less-than-ideal materials in most cases. The high-quality ones cost a pretty penny.

When using a trellis made of organic materials, take care not to jam the bottom into your soil too deep. It will rot much quicker when pressed against wet soil for a growing season. Once you're done with your trellis for the season, make sure to store it indoors to prevent deterioration.

BAMBOO TRELLISES

Bamboo is one of the cheapest, most environmentally friendly, and easiest to use vertical gardening material you'll ever come across. The uses for bamboo are practically endless. I think of it as the "Lego building block" of my vertical gardens.

You can do something as simple as sticking a few stakes in the ground and letting peas or other tendril-type climbers shoot up them or get fancy and create entire structures entirely out of bamboo.

For example, instead of buying a fancy (and expensive) trellis, why not make one out of bamboo sticks? All you need to do is secure the location where the crosspieces meet with some twine, twist ties, or zip ties. Bamboo trellises are incredible because you can customize them to your exact needs.

Bamboo trellises are fantastic when you need highly customized vertical gardening solutions.

A few pieces of bamboo and some twine lashing and you've got yourself a sturdy trellis.

Builder's Wire

Also known as wire remesh, cattle panel, or fence panel, builder's wire is a cheap way to build a trellis. It usually has 6-inch gaps between wires, making it easy to reach through and work with in the garden. Most hardware stores will either carry 5 × 10-foot sheets, or a 5 × 50- to 100-foot roll.

If you use builder's wire, make sure to pick up some bolt cutters so you can slice through the thick metal. You may also want to spray them with a coat of rust protectant, as in my experience these panels can rust quickly when exposed to the elements.

You can also lean unstructured trellises against fences for plants that don't require extreme amounts of support. This works very well for plants like cucumbers, as you can lean a trellis at a 45-degree angle against a fence and allow the cucumbers to fall through the trellis. Then, when it comes time to harvest, you simply snip under the trellis and you've got an instant meal.

A cucumber trellis is leaning at a 45-degree angle for easy access to gorgeous cukes.

Winter melons dangle down from a gorgeous arbor.

Arbors and Arches

The most awe-inspiring gardens I see often make use of arches, creating an edible "tunnel." It's an incredible feeling to be able to walk under hanging squashes, cucumbers, melons, peas, and more.

Arbors and arches are a more ambitious vertical gardening project, and I recommend simply buying one at a local garden center. They work well when used to bridge a garden path, each end inserted into a raised bed.

Fences

Growing on fences is a mixed bag due to the many ways fences are constructed. If you're lucky enough to have a fence with gaps, such as a chain-link fence, then your trellis is built already. Otherwise, you'll need to add supports to your fence to turn it into a vertical gardening masterpiece.

Heavy-Duty Modular Trellis

There are a million and one ways to make a trellis. The method you choose depends on the plants you're growing and how sturdy you want it to be. From pole beans to large squashes, this heavy-duty metal trellis can support just about anything. If you're not too handy, no sweat. This trellis requires no power tools, nails, or screws.

Step 2

Drive the rebar far enough into the soil to provide support. Add conduit pipe over the rebar to fasten the fence panel easier.

Be sure to install your trellis early in the season so your plants can climb up it naturally as they grow.

Step 3

Zip ties or twine makes this trellis easy to assemble . . . and disassemble.

Materials

- fence or cattle panel
- concrete rebar 6 feet long and ⅜ inch wide
- EMT conduit pipes, 10 feet long and ½ inch thick
- cable ties, 8 inches long

Steps

1. Position your fence panel where you want your trellis to be in the garden. This particular design is great up against the edge of a raised bed.

2. Position your rebar and press it into the ground *at least* 2 to 3 feet at the edges of the fence panel. Slide your conduit pipes onto the rebar and press firmly into the ground as well.

3. Secure your fence panel to the conduit with cable ties and trim off the loose ends with some snips when you're done.

4. If you're growing vining plants without the ability to climb on their own (such as tomatoes), you'll need to gently weave the growing tips through the fence panel as the plant grows. For natural climbers (beans, peas, and so on), you can sit back and let them find their way up the trellis naturally.

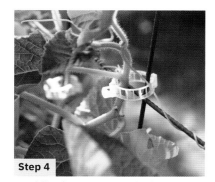

Step 4

Tendrils of a young squash plant twirl around the fence panel, supported by tomato clips.

Repurposed Hanging Shoe Rack

If you're tight on space, this is the project for you. Perfect even for the tiniest apartment, a repurposed hanging shoe organizer is a fantastic way to squeeze a *lot* of plants onto a patch of wall or fencing. The best part? The materials cost less than $20, far cheaper than most vertical gardening systems for sale.

Materials
- cheap hanging shoe rack
- screws or nails for hanging
- scissors
- potting soil
- transplants

Steps

1. Select a location for your shoe rack garden. Fences, sheds, and garages are great options, but you can also make this work on a sunny wall inside your home. Just be sure to screw it into some studs because it'll be holding soil, water, *and* plants.

2. Pour some water into one of the pouches to see how it drains. If the water pools up and stays in the pouch, poke some holes in the bottom with a pen or other sharp object to increase drainage.

3. Fill each pouch with potting mix, taking care to leave some space at the top so soil doesn't spill out of the pouch.

4. Add your transplants and top off with a bit of extra soil. Water them in well, checking for water spillage.

Optional: If you want to make your planter a bit prettier, add some plant labels or decorations.

Step 2

Make sure water drains from the pouches; that is crucial to making this project work.

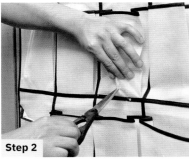

Step 2

For nonporous shoe racks, snip a few holes to let water drain.

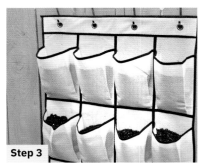

Step 3

Use the Epic Potting Mix recipe (see page 67) for best results.

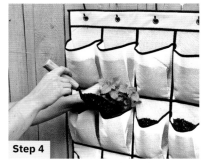

Step 4

Be sure to fill your pouches almost to the top, taking care to cover a plant's rootball.

Attractive, modular, and movable . . . what more can you ask for in a vertical garden?

Rain Gutter Garden

Rain gutters are one of the best vertical gardening materials you can use, and they're everywhere. No matter where you live, you should be able to get your hands on some cheap gutters to repurpose into a beautiful and functional fence or wall garden.

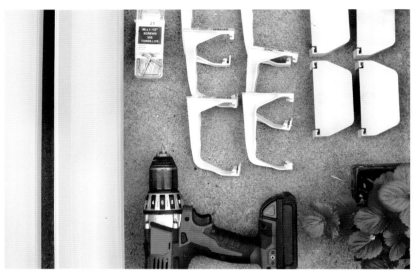

Most of what you'll need for your rain gutter garden can be found at a local hardware store.

Materials
- gutter hangers
- hanging screws
- drill and drill bits
- 10-foot rain gutters
- gutter end caps
- potting soil
- plants

Steps

1. Choose a south-, southeast-, or southwest-facing fence or wall if possible. If you want to grow shade-loving crops or simply don't have any other options, an east-, west-, or north-facing surface will work just fine.

No matter where you decide to locate your gutter garden, you should have a sturdy structure to drill into. These will be holding soil, water, and growing plants, so make sure you account for that. A good rule of thumb is to place them between two fence posts, each spaced at least 2 feet from the end of the gutters.

Take your gutter hangers and screw them into the support posts. Depending on your design decision, either hang level or offset. I've chosen to hang them level for this guide, but I love the look of offset hangers and they make excellent use of gravity as a drainage and watering mechanism.

2. You have two options for rain gutter placement. The option you choose will determine how to drill your drainage holes. The options are:
- Hang your gutters so they're level, and drill drainage holes throughout the gutter bottoms.
- Angle each gutter slightly to one side and drill drainage holes at the lower end.

3. Hang your gutters on the fasteners and attach each end cap, snapping them together.

4. Fill with your favorite potting mix (or make your own), and you're ready for planting.

5. Because gutters aren't very tall, you have to be selective about what you grow in this garden. Leafy greens such as lettuce, Asian greens, spinach, and mustard do very well. If you prefer root crops, then radishes and beets are your go-tos. If you want fruit, strawberries are the best crop for you. A few other ideas include smaller alliums such as chives or green onions, almost any herb, and snap peas.

Step 1

Screw your hangers into studs; you'll be putting a lot of weight in those rain gutters.

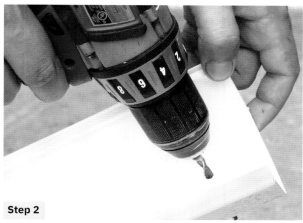

Step 2

Drainage holes drilled throughout your rain gutters help prevent root rot.

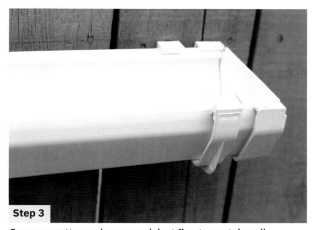

Step 3

Snap-on gutter end caps work just fine to contain soil and water.

Step 4

A standard potting mix with a bit of extra peat moss works well for rain gutters because they're so shallow.

Step 5

My final rain gutters have been interplanted with basil and strawberries.

5

Indoor Edibles

If you think you can't grow any-thing because you don't have any space outdoors, then think again. Indoor edible gardening is not only possible, it's simple. With a little creativity and an understanding of how to care for plants grown inside your home, you'll have bountiful harvests even if you live in a tiny apartment.

In this chapter, you'll learn:
- **How to audit your indoor space to maximize production**
- **Simple ways to grow herbs indoors**
- **A complete guide to growing nutrient-rich microgreens on autopilot**

This south-facing window gets a lot of light, so cramming in as many succulents as possible makes sense.

Audit Your Growing Space

Indoor gardens can take up as much or as little space as you are willing to sacrifice. If you're like me, it won't feel like much of a sacrifice at all. I squeeze plants into every corner of my living space and attempt to create an edible urban jungle, no matter where I live.

South-facing windowsills are the holy grail of indoor gardening, as you'll make the most use of available light. If you have a few, you can even make indoor cherry tomatoes, beans, or other smaller fruiting plants work.

Vertical shelving is a great option to make the most of a wall that gets bright light throughout the day without taking up too much floor space. In my own room, I repurposed a leaning bookshelf I found on Craigslist for about $20. It houses the only ornamental plants I grow, a beautiful collection of houseplants that brings a peaceful vibe to my bedroom.

Repurposed stepping stools or leaning bookshelves make excellent plant stands.

Herbs are one of the highest-value crops you can grow indoors on a per-pound basis.

Kitchen Herbs: Bring Some Spice to Your Home

One of my favorite things in my home is my kitchen herb garden. I have a thriving herb garden outside as well, but there's something amazing about cooking a homegrown meal and reaching right over the sink to grab some fresh basil, thyme, or oregano to spice up what's in the pan.

When starting a kitchen herb garden, be honest with yourself about *what you actually like to use in the kitchen*. When I first started gardening, I grew everything under the sun because it seemed like "that's what a gardener is supposed to grow." Well, after a year of growing and not using the sage in my kitchen garden, I finally said "goodbye" to that herb.

Never feel like you "have" to grow something. Grow what you like.

Mason Jar Herb Garden

Mason jar projects are a tried-and-true indoor gardening staple. They're made from commonly found materials, are easy to build, and can be transported around the house with ease.

This herb garden can be placed on a windowsill, in a bay window, or mounted on a board and hung on the wall with the use of some hose clamps.

Step 1

Although it's not necessary, pebbles can protect your soil if you end up overwatering your jars.

The best part of Mason jar gardens is their portability; you can move them to where the light is in your home.

Materials
- wide-mouth Mason jars
- gravel or stone pebbles
- horticultural charcoal (optional)
- potting soil
- herb seeds or seedlings
- plant labels (optional)

If you want to hang your Mason jars, you'll need:
- wooden board
- drill
- screws
- hose clamps
- cable staples
- hammer

Steps

1. Your first step is to fill your jars. Mason jars don't have drainage holes at the bottom of them, so place ½ to 1 inch of stone pebbles at the bottom to help prevent overwatering. If you want, mix those with horticultural charcoal to help stabilize soil pH and prevent bacteria buildup.

2. Fill your jars with soil and either sow seeds or transplant herb seedlings. Make sure to cover the roots up well and break up the roots a bit so they can expand into the Mason jar. Label the jars if you like.

3. These little gardens are easy to care for, as the jars are clear and it's easy to see when they need watering. Harvest early and harvest often to prevent them from getting out of hand. Don't be afraid to rip old herb plants out and replace them with new ones as they start to develop flowers or look old and decrepit.

If you're hanging these Mason jars on the wall:
Place a wooden board on the wall and secure it, preferably to studs in the wall. Take your hose clamps and align them on the board, then attach them with your cable staples using a hammer.

Step 2

Leave 1 inch of room before transplanting in order to cover up the rootball with additional potting soil.

Step 2

You can start seeds directly in your Mason jars, but transplants will give your garden a head start as well.

Microgreens are one of my absolute favorite things to grow in small spaces.

Microgreens: Nature's Little Secret

If you haven't heard of microgreens, you're in for a treat. They've been absolutely *exploding* in the culinary scene, making appearances atop fancy dishes, soups, and salads at high-end restaurants.

What if I told you that you could grow these "fancy" greens at home? Better yet, that growing microgreens is *the easiest* way to get started growing edibles in small spaces?

What Are Microgreens, Anyway?

The name "microgreens" sounds a bit like it came straight out of an agriculture lab, but the truth is much simpler. Microgreens are just normal plants, except they're harvested at a *much* younger date than most edibles. They're sprouted and grown until their first set of "true leaves," which are the first leaves that develop *after* the seed leaves (called cotyledons) that emerge from the seed itself. If you've seen packages of baby spinach at the store, rewind the clock a few weeks and you can imagine what "micro-spinach" would look like.

If you're in cramped quarters but are still itching to grow something, these delicious (and nutritious) greens are the easiest way to start working on your green thumb. You can grow an entire tray of microgreens (enough for two to three salads) in fourteen days and a little over a square foot of space.

Essential Microgreen Materials

There are a few key materials you'll need to ensure microgreen growing success. At the most basic, you need seeds, trays, and soil.

WHERE DO I GET BULK SEEDS?

Because we plant so densely when growing microgreens, you'll go through *far* more seed. Seed packets start to look a bit expensive, so it makes sense to buy in bulk. See page 218 for some of the suppliers I recommend.

If you're just getting started growing microgreens, buying a few seed packets is okay. Once you find the microgreens you love growing, upgrade to buying bulk seed to save some cash.

MICROGREEN TRAYS

Technically, anything that holds soil and water can be used to grow microgreens. You can use anything you have lying around the house, such as cups, egg cartons, old plastic containers—the list goes on.

But if you want to get the industry standard microgreens growing gear, you'll want to go with 10×20-inch propagation trays. Each crop of microgreens you grow will require two trays, because you'll be flipping one over and using it as a blackout and humidity dome while your seeds are germinating.

SOIL

Microgreens don't require much nutrition from the soil. You harvest them *so* early in their life span that they get most of the nutrients they need from the seed itself. That being said, I find it's easier to grow them in soil than in a hydroponic growing medium.

A standard potting mix will work just fine, or you can mix your own based on some of the recipes in this book. The biggest consideration is the particle size of your soil. Avoid large pebbles, shredded bark, and other large particles, as they disrupt the even growth of your microgreens. If you can sift your soil through a ¼-inch screen, that's even better. It'll ensure you have soft, light, and fluffy soil.

A "field" of radish microgreens is ready for harvest.

Standard 1020 propagation trays make excellent microgreen growing containers.

Growing Microgreens from Start to Finish

Most microgreens are ready to harvest in around eight to fourteen days, so this is a short process. There aren't too many moving parts.

Preparing Your Tray

Before you sow your seeds, you need to prepare your growing tray. Moisten the soil and add it to your tray, filling to just below the brim. Filling further makes it harder for you to harvest. Make sure the soil surface is evenly smooth.

Tip: Adding water to the bottom of the tray *then* adding your soil makes it easier to have evenly moist soil.

Sowing Your Microgreens Seeds

It's time to plant. The size of your seeds will determine how much you need to plant. For most varieties of greens, around 1 ounce of seed is the perfect amount. For larger seeds, such as radish, pea, and sunflower, you'll need 2 to 4 ounces of seed to cover the tray.

Make sure you get as close to even coverage as you can. If you are planting something such as basil, which has extremely small seeds, you'll need to be especially careful about your coverage. For larger seeds such as radish or cabbage, you may need to sow more than you think. Remember that even though they may be large, a seed still only sprouts into one microgreen. (Unless you're growing beet or chard.)

After you've sown your seeds, mist them generously with water from a spray bottle.

Tip: To Soak or Not to Soak?

It's no secret that soaking your seeds speeds germination, but is it necessary when growing microgreens? For peas and sunflowers, yes. For everything else, I wouldn't worry about it; your seeds will do just fine sprinkled on the soil surface.

Blacking Out the Tray

For proper germination, your freshly planted microgreen seeds need a warm and dark place. Grab another growing tray and flip it over on top of your planted tray. Make sure that no light is leaking through, then put it in an area of the house that stays at about 70°F.

The Germination Phase

At this point, you have planted your seeds and they should be covered in a blackout dome. All you need to do now is mist your seeds every twelve hours or so for the first three to four days while they germinate. Feel free to peek under the hood; it won't harm them to check on their progress every now and then.

With the blackout dome on, your seeds are going to be very moist and ideally in a warm spot. If you have a hard time finding a warm area, look into purchasing a seedling heat mat. Keep in mind that optimal germination temperatures for most plants is anywhere from 65° to 85°F.

You might be wondering, "How long should I keep the blackout dome on?" Great question. The answer is, "It depends." Aim for about three to four days after your seeds germinate. Because no light is hitting the plants at this stage, they won't be undergoing any photosynthesis, so they're going to look kind of weak and pale. That's okay, as long as you don't let it go on too long.

Adding 4 cups of water to the bottom of the tray before adding your soil is an efficient way to pre-moisten it.

Spread your seed as evenly as possible to avoid overly dense growth in parts of your tray.

Your seeds need a bit of moisture to trigger the germination process.

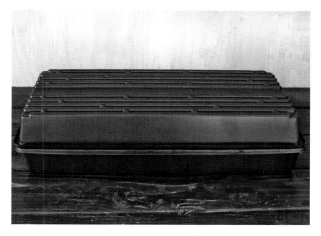

Another 1020 propagation tray that's flipped upside down works perfectly as a blackout dome.

Radish microgreens after a couple of days of exposure to light.

Enter the Light

After your seeds have sprouted and spent a few days in utter darkness, it's time to take them out of solitary confinement and into the light. This is what separates microgreens from sprouts; they're allowed to absorb light and actually grow past the cotyledon stage (the "seed leaves" of the plant).

In this phase, put your trays in an area that gets natural air circulation or supplement air circulation with a fan. In order to avoid common microgreen problems, air circulation is an absolute must. I ruined many trays of microgreens back when I started by ignoring this simple tip.

Be sure to mist your trays a few times a day to make sure they are well watered. Because microgreens are so delicate, allowing your tray to dry out will cause the stems to lose their strength fast. While you can add water to save them, they will not look the same, and we all want delicious and beautiful greens, right?

Make sure to water your trays once a day, preferably from the bottom, to avoid any mold or fungus issues from misting or top-watering.

To make harvesting and cleaning easier, run your hand across the tops of your microgreens to brush off all the seed shells. Trust me; it saves a lot of time.

Harvesting and Washing

The harvesting process is simple but crucial. You can either create a headache for yourself or make it a smooth, easy process by following a few simple guidelines.

First, use an extremely sharp knife or pair of large scissors to harvest. Grip the microgreens lightly with one hand and slice off in bunches. Leave around ¼ to ½ inch of stem at the bottom to avoid harvesting soil, seed husks, or poorly germinated greens.

Once you've harvested your tray, inspect your microgreens. If you have clean greens without any dirt, seed hulls, or other debris, I recommend *not* washing them. Washing will reduce the shelf life of your microgreens by 20 to 30 percent.

If you want to be safe or you've got some dirt in your harvest, toss your microgreens into a colander lined with a paper towel. Fill with water and jostle the micros around to free them of dirt and seed hulls. Then toss them into a lined salad spinner and give them a healthy spin. The goal is to remove as much moisture as possible.

After spinning, spread them out on a counter on a paper towel to air-dry; then transfer to a container lined with a damp paper towel for storage in the fridge. If you follow this process to the letter, your microgreens won't go soggy in the fridge and will last about a week.

Make sure not to pull up any extra debris when harvesting; it makes washing your microgreens a headache.

How to Solve Common Microgreen Problems

I've gotten hundreds of emails about microgreen growing problems over the years. Here are the most common problems you'll run into when growing your precious microgreens, as well as tried-and-true solutions.

Root hairs are forming from these newly germinated cress seeds.

Spiderweb-like white mold has formed on top of moist soil.

Mold or Fungus

Mold is one of the biggest problems I've run into due to the 70°F-plus summer temperatures and high humidity in my climate. First of all, there is a *big* difference between mold and root hairs, which are often confused for mold.

Root hairs are concentrated around the main root of an individual seedling, radiating outward in straightish lines. They're vital to the early development of your microgreens and shouldn't be disturbed.

Mold, on the other hand, looks like a spiderweb crawling across the surface of your soil. It starts out in one area in a small, wispy ball and then expands quickly over the growing media. If you don't take care of it, pretty soon it will climb up the stems of your plants, and your entire crop is ruined. Here are the four causes of mold in your microgreens:

- **Bad airflow**—Place a fan near your trays to gently blow air over them.
- **High humidity**—Remove the blackout dome earlier or use a fan to decrease local humidity.
- **Too warm or too cold**—Try to keep your growing environment around 70° to 75°F. If it's too warm, you create a good environment for mold growth; if it's too cold, then moisture sits on the soil longer, causing issues as well.
- **Hygiene**—Never use tools you haven't sterilized with a disinfecting solution, and always sterilize your trays.

Solutions

Spray or soak your trays in a sterilizing mixture made up of:

- 6⅓ cups water
- 3½ tablespoons white vinegar
- 3½ tablespoons food-grade hydrogen peroxide

If you *already* have mold on your micros, then do the following:

- Increase air circulation by using a fan or by moving them to a breezy area.
- Decrease the amount of seed you sow per tray to give seedlings more space.
- Treat with a few drops of grapeseed extract mixed with water.

Slow Germination

The length of time it takes your microgreens to germinate will depend on the type of plants you're growing. But if you're experiencing extremely slow germination, you either have bad seed or an environmental issue on your hands.

Solutions

If you are experiencing slow germination of your micros, then try the following:

- Spray more often to increase moisture.
- Make sure your trays are in at least 70°F growing environment.
- Confirm your seeds are viable by doing a germination test with a wet paper towel.

Yellowish Microgreens

It's completely natural for your microgreens to be yellow once you take off the blackout dome. After all, they haven't been exposed to light, so they haven't had the chance to photosynthesize. But if your greens aren't so green even *after* exposing them to light, you need to double-check a few things.

Solutions

If you observe yellowing microgreens, then try the following:

- Place your trays near a stronger light source.
- For future plantings, take the blackout dome off your trays earlier.

Clumpy Microgreens

Sometimes it's difficult to spread your seeds evenly in your trays. If you plant seeds too close together they will begin to clump. This is doubly true if you're growing a mucilaginous seed such as basil, because that type forms a gel coating that makes it even easier to stick to other seeds.

Clumping is a problem because when your seeds sprout, a few of the seedlings will "push" the rest of them up into the air, suspending their roots and possibly bringing dirt along with them.

Solutions

If you find your microgreens are clumping, do the following:

- Decrease the total seed volume planted per tray.
- Spread seeds more evenly throughout the tray.

Weak-Looking Microgreens

This is an all-encompassing condition that covers the rest of the problems that you'll have. It's hard to troubleshoot exactly why a particular microgreen crop is doing poorly if you've already made sure you don't have any of the conditions described.

In my case, a lot of the weaknesses I see in my crops is due to a lack of moisture control; it's either too dry or too wet. In some cases, I didn't properly prepare the seeds before planting them, and in others I took the blackout dome off too early or too late.

Solutions

If you find your microgreens look weak, ask yourself if you're doing the following:

- Read the seed packets carefully to see if there are special considerations for a particular plant.
- Stick to a normal watering and misting schedule.
- Different crops need the blackout dome taken off at different times; be sure to be crop-specific.
- Some crops need the blackout dome flipped upside down on top of them to make them "struggle" to thrive.

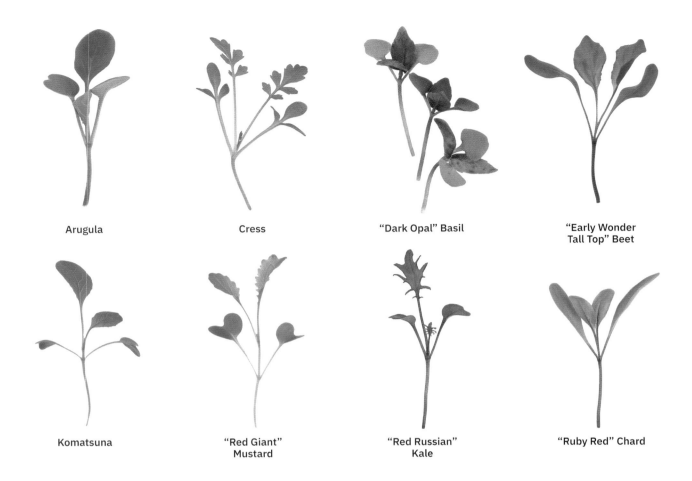

Arugula

Cress

"Dark Opal" Basil

"Early Wonder Tall Top" Beet

Komatsuna

"Red Giant" Mustard

"Red Russian" Kale

"Ruby Red" Chard

Which Microgreens Should I Grow?

There are over sixty varieties of plants that are commonly cultivated as microgreens, but many of these are either rare or expensive when buying bulk seed. On top of that, some microgreens are *much* harder to grow than others.

I've compiled a list of some of the most popular microgreens to grow for beginners, in order of their difficulty. If you're just starting out, try some at the top of the following chart and work your way down as you gain more experience.

Store freshly harvested microgreens in a glass jar with a lid. Don't pack them in tightly.

In a sealed glass jar your microgreens will keep for at least a week if refrigerated. But you should always try to eat them when they are at their freshest.

Microgreens	Soak?	Seed (oz)	Blackout (days)	Germination (days)	Harvest (days)
Arugula	No	1	4–6	2–3	8–12
Cabbage	No	1	3–4	1–2	8–12
Kale	No	1	3–5	2–3	8–12
Lettuce	No	1	3–5	2–3	10–12
Sunflower	Yes	9	2–3	2–3	8–12
Wheatgrass	Yes	16	2	1–2	8–10
Peas	Yes	12	3–5	2–3	8–12
Basil	No	1	5–7	3–4	10–15
Beet	No	1.5	6–8	3–4	10–12

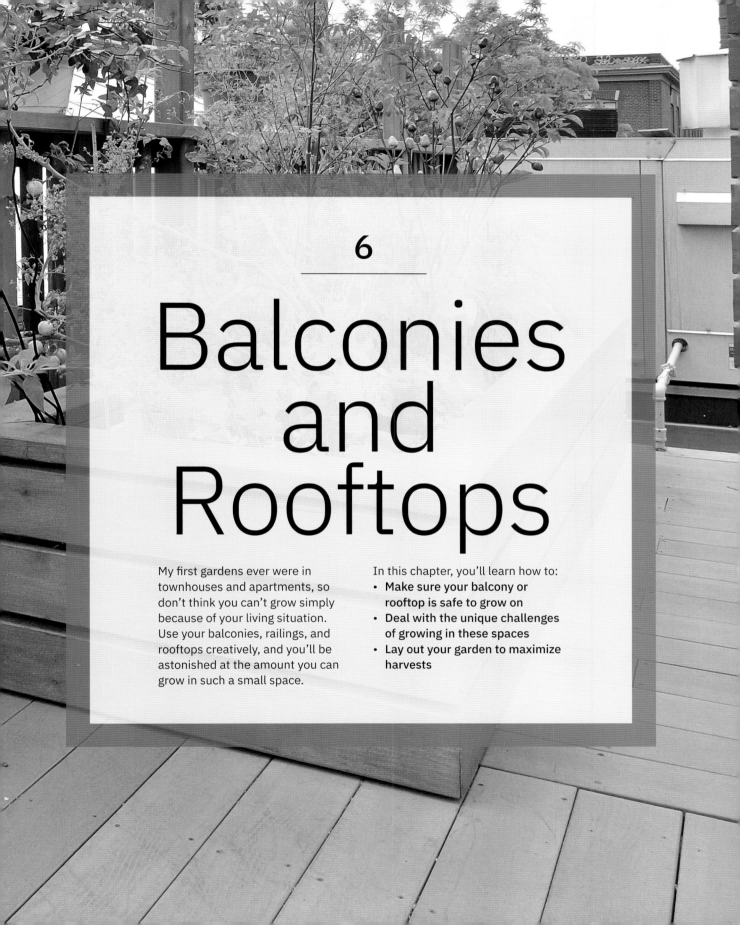

6

Balconies and Rooftops

My first gardens ever were in townhouses and apartments, so don't think you can't grow simply because of your living situation. Use your balconies, railings, and rooftops creatively, and you'll be astonished at the amount you can grow in such a small space.

In this chapter, you'll learn how to:
- **Make sure your balcony or rooftop is safe to grow on**
- **Deal with the unique challenges of growing in these spaces**
- **Lay out your garden to maximize harvests**

In smaller living spaces, balcony gardens may be your only access to outdoor urban gardening.

Balcony Gardening

Besides the obvious advantages for your plants, there are plenty of benefits to balcony gardening that are often overlooked.

Before I became a gardener, balconies were always a place to sit for a few minutes and then go back inside. I had nothing exciting to do on the balcony besides flip through some pages of a book or have a quick meal. Once I started growing my own food, I never looked at balconies the same way again. All I see is *growing potential*.

By growing on your balcony, you're beautifying a space that's otherwise pretty drab. On top of that, you're able to accomplish these things:

- reduce noise pollution by growing living barricades
- make it harder for pests to reach your garden
- provide a bit of food for yourself and reduce your "food miles"

Planning Your Balcony Jungle

Your first major consideration when growing on a balcony is whether the balcony itself can support what you're growing. Most balconies should be able to handle a few containers or beds, but it's a good idea to test the sturdiness of your space before you start loading it up with plants.

You'd be surprised at how heavy a container can get once it's full of soil, water, and a loaded tomato plant, especially if you have a bunch of them. Spread your pots around your balcony instead of clumping them in one area. Doing this will spread out the weight distribution and you won't have any nasty balcony gardening mishaps.

Next, take stock of the growing conditions on your balcony.

SUN

What direction does your balcony face? South-facing balconies are the best, but southeast- or southwest-facing will do. And if you've got a north-facing window, you can still grow plants. You'll just need to adjust the types you grow to be shade-loving varieties.

SHADE

I recommend going out on the balcony in the morning, afternoon, and evening to see how the shadows fall on the space before setting up your garden. Oftentimes you'll set up a balcony garden only to find that you placed your plants in an area that gets shaded by an obstruction for 80 percent of the day. Take note of how shade plays over your balcony to help inform the best location to set up your garden.

WIND

Wind issues are the biggest problem with balcony gardens, far more so than for raised beds or containers on the ground. Your first option is to plant wind-tolerant plants, such as rosemary. A second option with more flexibility is to stake your plants well and use windscreens to help break some of the nastier gusts.

Similar to checking the shade on your balcony, walk out a few times during the day to see which way the wind is blowing as well as how strong the gusts are. If you get a lot of wind, make sure you use heavier-duty pots, such as terra-cotta.

Rainwater is free of city water additives and reduces pressure on storm drains.

WATER DRAINAGE

Most balconies have drainage holes, or at the very least are sloped so water runs in a specific direction. Check this when you're growing on a balcony; the last thing you want to do is annoy a downstairs neighbor by raining dirty water all over them every time you water the garden.

If you live in an area that gets a lot of rain, you can earn extra conservation points by installing a balcony rain barrel. This way you prevent massive amounts of runoff from being wasted and get to water your garden with fresh rainwater, which is always preferable to using city water.

Even the smallest balconies can be designed creatively to include productive greenery.

Don't be afraid to litter your balcony floor with plants.

Balcony Design Ideas

Every balcony is unique, so the urban gardening masterpiece you decide to create should be tailored to your situation. That being said, there are some basic rules of thumb to follow to create a balcony garden that's beautiful, functional, and, best of all—*productive*.

Balconies have three distinct sections to consider, which are the floor, the railing, and everything else. Thinking in these three layers will help you make the absolute best use of the limited space you have.

Sit-on-top planters make great use of railing space but be careful if you get a lot of wind.

For those windier spots, secure your planters with decking screws.

There are many variations of attachment-style planters, so be sure to choose one that fits your railing.

FLOOR

If you're willing to sacrifice some foot room, the floor of your balcony is a great spot for larger containers full of plants that need a bit of space to grow. Tomatoes, peppers, eggplants, and beans are all great plants to grow in containers on your balcony floor. Over time, they'll fill out the space well.

BALCONY RAILING PLANTERS

Your railings are the *crème de la crème* location in your balcony garden. They're exposed to the most sun and don't take up extra space as they hang *off* the balcony. In a growing space that's already so limited, this is a godsend.

For all their value, there is no more confusing piece of gardening gear than balcony railing planters. Because there are so many different types of railings, it's often confusing exactly how to attach planters to railings. Given the amount of wind that balconies are subject to, the last thing you want to do is shoddily attach a railing planter only to see it tumbling down to the ground below.

Sit-on-Top Planters

If your railings are a standard size, you can often pick up planters that have a notched bottom of exactly that size. These are great options if you want to go with a plug-and-play option. All you'll need to do is plop some soil in them, pot them up with plants, and start growing.

If your balcony gets a fair amount of wind, these may not be the best choice, as they can blow off, especially when the soil gets dry and the planter gets lighter. Choose a different option if your balcony gets blasted by the elements.

Screw-on-Top Planters

These types are the same as the sit on tops, but they don't have a notched bottom. These are screwed directly into the railing, so they're great for wood.

Attachment-Style Planters

These are the most common type of railing planters, and they have a hook design to place around the railing. The planter then rests on its own weight, pressing into the side of the railing. They're great options if you *know* that the design will fit your railing.

Because so many different railing designs exist, it's hard to tell at first whether one of these will fit your balcony. I recommend measuring the width of your railing and comparing it to the size of the hook or attachment on the planter box.

Hanging baskets can produce an overwhelming amount of food, right above your head.

HANGING GARDENS

Oftentimes the best space to grow on your balcony is right above your head. Hanging baskets are an exceptional way to make good visual use of the balcony, as well as packing in some extra herbs, veggies, or fruits.

There are a multitude of different hanging basket designs—plastic with reservoirs, wicker, wire-framed . . . the list goes on. No matter which style you choose, make sure you choose one that's large enough to support what you're growing.

The liner you use for your hanging container matters quite a bit. Remember, you're growing plants above your head. The last thing you want to do is have a bunch of soil and water dumped on you as you enjoy your morning coffee.

Nothing beats walking onto the balcony in the morning to pick fresh strawberries from an overhead basket.

Common liners for hanging baskets include:

- **Peat moss**—a thick, inert liner that looks amazing in a hanging basket, but can be a bit annoying to work with.
- **Coco coir**—usually comes pre-fitted to baskets you purchase at a local nursery or big-box store. Retains water well but can look a little unkempt after prolonged growing.
- **Burlap**—cheap and can be cut to size to retrofit existing containers. Retains much less water than peat moss and coco coir.

There are plants that shouldn't be grown in hanging baskets. Anything that spreads like crazy or requires a lot of maintenance (like root crops) aren't good fits for hanging baskets. You don't want to keep pulling down your baskets to care for your plants, so choose low-maintenance crops.

When planting in your baskets, keep in mind that different plants mature at different rates, and try to group plants that grow similarly for easy harvesting and care.

One of my absolute favorite hanging-basket plants for balconies is the strawberry. Not only are plants often sold at the nursery in an existing basket, but they also grow extremely well in hanging containers. There's nothing like walking out on the balcony with a bowl of oatmeal and topping it with fresh strawberries you pick by reaching right above your head.

Making Balcony Garden Care Easy

Balcony gardening is attractive *because* it's such an easy method to get started with, but the following are a few tips that make it an absolute breeze.

SEEDLINGS, NOT SEEDS

It's easier to get your garden off to a good start if you buy seedlings from a local nursery and simply transplant them into your balcony garden. Starting seeds is certainly a fun option to try if you want to flex your gardening muscles. But if you're a first-time gardener looking to get growing fast, I'd shamelessly buy seedlings from a local nursery.

BIGGER CONTAINERS = BETTER

The biggest downfall of growing in containers on a balcony is just that . . . you're growing in containers. They dry out quickly, especially if you're using terra-cotta pots. To counteract this and give your plants the even moisture that they need, select the largest pots you can. The increased volume will allow the soil to hold more water and evaporate much more slowly.

SELF-WATERING CONTAINERS

One step above choosing larger containers is choosing larger containers that are self-watering. These containers wick water from a chamber at the bottom of the pot to give your plants' roots a consistent supply. You can find large self-watering containers at most nurseries or big-box stores, or you can build your own using the plans in this book. The extra cost is well worth the time you'll save watering your plants.

MULCH

Don't be afraid to mulch your balcony containers. Gravel and micro-bark are both good options and will keep the sun off of the soil, which keeps your plants' roots cool and able to retain more water. Mulching is especially helpful if you're growing in long shallow containers.

WATER-RETAINING GRANULES

If you're having an impossible time keeping your soil moist, you might be tempted to use water-retaining granules in your potting mix. These polymers swell to many times their original size and hold onto a ton of water.

However, I'd caution against this. Most of these granules are made from polyacrylamides, which eventually break down over time, reducing their effectiveness. Studies have also shown them not to affect plant health positively and, in fact, sometimes reduce plant health.

That's to say nothing of the potentially harmful effects of polyacrylamides as they break down over the years. My recommendation is to practice good gardening techniques such as mulching, observing your soil, and making watering part of your daily routine instead of resorting to quick fixes such as this one.

Easy Crops for Balcony Gardens

The only true requirement for a balcony garden is that you don't grow anything that will absolutely take over the space. Sprawling squash plants, for example, wouldn't be the best choice. That being said, even squash is *possible*.

However, there are some plants that are better suited for beautifying a balcony, as listed in the table below.

Choose the biggest containers you can fit and manage on your balcony, especially if you are growing thirsty crops like tomatoes.

Plant	Varieties
Herbs	Basil, sage, thyme, oregano, and so on
Leafy greens	Loose leaf lettuce, spinach, kale, and so on
Garlic	'Artichoke', 'Silverskin'
Tomato	'Patio Princess', 'Balcony'
Lettuce	'Green Oak Leaf', 'Black Seeded Simpson'
Peppers	'Camelot'
Eggplant	'Fairy Tale', 'Bambino'
Swiss chard	'Rhubard', 'Rainbow'
Beans	'Blue Lake' (pole), 'Purple Queen' (bush)
Cucumber	'Spacemaster 80'
Strawberry	'Ozark Beauty', 'Seascape'

The overly cluttered look can sometimes coalesce into a wonderful and productive aesthetic.

Rooftop Gardening

If you're lucky enough to have a rooftop deck, a whole world of urban gardening options is available to you.

Why Grow on Your Rooftop?

Aside from the obvious benefits as an urban gardener, there are some shockingly important environmental gains to be had from rooftop growing. More greenery on rooftops helps capture water, meaning less pressure on city sewer systems. You might not think this is a big deal, but remember this: Most cities are covered in nonporous concrete. Water *never* seeps into the ground, thereby causing runoff into the sewer and increased pressure on our water treatment systems.

Another important benefit is mitigation of the "heat island" effect. This is a phenomenon where built-up areas are often much hotter than more rural, less-developed areas. The difference can be from 1.8° to 5.4°F in the daytime, which doesn't sound like much. But in the evening that difference can be up to 22°F as the pavement, roofing, and concrete release stored heat.

Introducing plants to your rooftop brings back more than just some greenery—beneficial insects, bees, and birds can all come back and create a truly natural oasis, often several floors above the soil.

Is Your Rooftop a Suitable Growing Space?

Unfortunately, not all rooftops are built to support a garden. On top of that, your HOA, local regulations, or landlord (if you're renting) might not be too keen on the project. Before you get started, here are some things to consider.

MICROCLIMATES

We've already addressed your USDA Hardiness Zone in the "How to Know What to Plant . . . and When to Plant It" section of the book (see page 28). As mentioned in that section, your climate is influenced by local geography and the specific conditions of your growing space. This is doubly true for rooftops, which are often exposed to a great deal of sun, wind, and higher temperatures than the average in-ground garden.

One of your biggest considerations with rooftops is where shadows fall throughout the day. If you're in the shadow of a large high-rise for half of your day, that fact heavily affects what you can grow. Take stock of the buildings, trees, walls, and structures around you. It's a good idea to check in the morning, afternoon, and evening to see how the shadows play out over your potential growing space. It might seem like a chore, but this up-front work can save you a season's worth of growing headaches in the future.

The opposite of shadows, *hot spots* are areas on your rooftop that are unnaturally hot due to the building materials being a heat sink or reflections from nearby buildings casting more light than expected on an area. When you're surveying your roof for shadows, keep in mind hot spots as well.

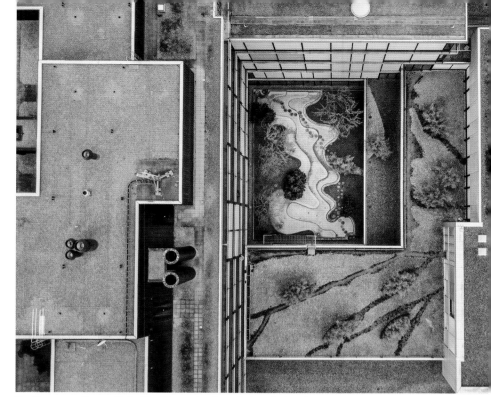

Rooftops aren't usually built with garden installs in mind, so be sure to audit your roof.

No matter how flat you think your roof is, it has a slight slope. Similar to balconies, roofs need water to flow away somehow. Over time, roofs also develop "pools" where water will collect. Keep an eye out for these the next time it rains in your area.

Finally, you have wind to consider. Wind is often much stronger on a rooftop than on a balcony due to its higher location. The higher your garden is, the more wind will be a factor. Sit outside and get a sense of how strong the winds can be, especially during a rainstorm. Consider the direction and force; these will inform how you should support your plants as they grow.

If you're growing on a rooftop deck or structure already designed for human use, then your roof is likely in good shape to start planting. However, if you're planning on building any larger, heavier beds, then consider consulting a structural engineer. It might seem like overkill, but the last thing you want is for your roof to cave in during your quest to grow some epic vegetables.

A structural engineer can examine your blueprints and building and give you both the dead load capacity (the weight of the roof itself and all permanent fixtures) and the live load capacity (additional weight added by people, beds, pots, rain barrels, etc.). You can use these figures to determine exactly what to build when it comes to your rooftop green paradise.

A QUICK WORD ON BUILDING CODES

While the codes that apply to your particular building will be unique to you and your local municipality, there are a few general ones to keep an eye out for:

- **Access Points**—Access points are the entry and exit points of your rooftop. Most cities require them to be constructed a certain way, as well as require that a rooftop garden be a certain distance from the access point.
- **No-Build Zones**—You usually can't build structures right on the edge of your building. If you're in a condo complex with an HOA, you'll often be pestered about how your railings and rooftop looks from the street level as well. It's always a good idea to check those requirements.

High-density plantings are in neatly laid-out raised beds—all on top of a roof.

ROOF STRUCTURE

Generally speaking, rooftops are meant to protect you from the elements, not to house wine barrels of potatoes, buckets of tomatoes, or cucumbers on large trellises. You'll need to give your rooftop a once-over to see if it can structurally support what you plan to grow.

Large planter boxes augmented with vertical trellises grow vining veggies. *Credit: Jeannie Phan of Studio Plants*

Laying Out Your Rooftop Garden

When designing any garden, it's a good idea to get out a pen and paper and start sketching. There's something about seeing a top-down view of your space that helps clarify what to grow and where to grow it.

With your rooftop garden, this top-down view is doubly important because of some of the unique challenges presented by rooftops. You have to consider the structure of the roof and any obstacles, and determine which methods you'll use to cultivate crops.

This rooftop garden makes extensive use of drip irrigation to get the watering job done.

WATERING

You'll also need to consider how you're getting water up to the rooftop. Most roofs don't have built-in irrigation, meaning you have a few options.

Hand Watering

This is the best option for most rooftop growers. Whether you're using a hose or a can, hand watering gets you into the garden at least once a day to observe and care for your plants. You'll pick up on the little nuances of each crop over the course of its life and build your skills as a gardener along the way.

Drip Irrigation

Drip irrigation is a personal favorite of mine due to its simplicity and automation, but it can lead to garden neglect if you don't make it a habit to spend time in the garden every single day. It's a bit of a learning process to set up drip irrigation for the first time, so opt for a prebuilt kit that comes with all of the pieces you'll need.

Rainwater Irrigation

If you're in an area with good rainfall, you can set up rain barrels and irrigate the garden directly from the captured water. First, check to see whether you're allowed to collect rainwater in your area. And also check whether the rainwater you collect isn't also collecting harmful compounds from your roof.

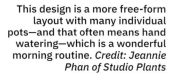

This design is a more free-form layout with many individual pots—and that often means hand watering—which is a wonderful morning routine. *Credit: Jeannie Phan of Studio Plants*

7

Hydroponics

Hydroponics is the practice of growing plants using only water, nutrients, and a growing medium. The word "hydroponics" comes from the root words *hydro*, meaning water, and *ponos*, meaning labor. To put it bluntly, hydroponics is a method of growing where the water does all of the work.

Sounds high tech and futuristic, right? You might be surprised to learn that the earliest examples of hydroponics date back to the Hanging Gardens of Babylon and the Floating Gardens of China. Humans have used these techniques for thousands of years.

History of Hydroponics

The earliest modern reference to hydroponics was by a man named William Frederick Gericke. While working at the University of California, Berkeley, he began to popularize the idea that plants could be grown in a solution of nutrients and water instead of soil.

Naturally, the general public, as well as Gericke's colleagues, doubted this claim. He quickly proved them wrong by growing 25-foot-high tomato vines using only water and nutrients.

He decided to call this growing method *hydroponics*. The shocking results of Gericke's experiment with tomatoes prompted further research into the field. More research was performed by University of California scientists who uncovered a great many benefits related to soilless plant cultivation.

Why Grow in a Hydroponic System?

One of the biggest advantages that hydroponics has over growing in soil is water conservation. When growing plants in soil, some water will always be lost to evaporation or simply not be taken up by the plants' root zones. On top of that, if you give your plant too much water, its roots won't be able to get enough oxygen. Give it too little, and it can quickly dry out and die.

Hydroponics solves this watering conundrum in a few different ways.

1. Oxygenation. First, the water reservoir can be constantly oxygenated, making sure that a plant's roots obtain the optimum level of oxygen. The plant's root system no longer has soil surrounding it, blocking oxygen uptake by the roots.

2. Less Water. Second, hydroponics uses much less water than growing in soil because water can be recirculated. In traditional gardening, water is poured over the ground and seeps into the soil. Only a small fraction of the water actually gets used by the plant. You can mitigate this by using drip irrigation or mulching, but the fact remains that some water is always lost. Hydroponics allows for the unused water to be recycled back into the system's reservoir, ready for use in the future. If you live in a hot, dry climate, this is a *massive* benefit.

3. Total Control. The last major benefit of hydroponics is the amount of control you have over your environment. When growing outside, you're at the mercy of the elements. One bad day can wipe out your garden if you're not careful. And that's saying nothing of pest and disease issues.

With hydroponics, battling pests and diseases is *much* easier. In most cases, your growing environment is portable, space efficient, and raised off of the ground. This makes it hard for bugs to reach your plants. Any soil-related diseases are rare in hydroponics as well. Lastly, you can control the climate completely with indoor grow lights, fans, and ventilation.

Fundamental Hydroponic Principles

Before I get into the different types of hydroponic systems and show you how to build your own, it's important to get a few basic principles out of the way. Growing plants hydroponically is a more scientific approach than growing in soil, so understanding these key principles are absolutely necessary before I get into the DIY system builds.

The Importance of Water

In addition to the normal functions water plays in gardening, water acts as the "container" around your plants' roots in a hydroponic system. Because of this, we have to dig a bit deeper and understand some of the finer details behind our world's most precious resource.

EC, TDS, AND PPM

I know what you're thinking. More acronyms? I promise these are the last ones you'll need to learn for now, but they're exceptionally important. Just as your water needs to be in the right pH range, it also needs the right amount of nutrients to feed your plants.

Too little, and your plants suffer from nutrient deficiencies of all kinds, leading to a slow death. Too much, and you put your plants at risk for *nutrient burn*, where your plants cannot handle the abundance of nutrients and the leaves begin to turn yellow and crispy.

But how do we measure the amount of nutrients in our water? This is where EC, TDS, and PPM come into the picture. This can get confusing, so I'll lay it out for you as simply as possible.

Electrical Conductivity (EC)

Electrical conductivity seems like a weird thing to measure when it comes to your nutrients, but it makes sense upon closer inspection. Pure water doesn't conduct electricity, but when we add nutrients (also known as mineral ions), water becomes more and more conductive. EC is a measure of how conductive your nutrient solution is, and by proxy how much nutrient you've added to your water.

Total Dissolved Solids (TDS) and Parts Per Million (PPM)

As its name implies, total dissolved solids is a measure of the concentration of dissolved solids in your nutrient reservoir. This sounds like a more sensible way to measure the amount of nutrients in your solution, right?

It's more complicated than that. A meter that gives you a TDS reading is *actually* measuring EC and then converting it into a *parts per million* (PPM) reading. PPM is straightforward; it tells you how much of your nutrient solution *isn't* water. For example, a PPM of 800 means that 800 out of 1,000,000 parts of the solution are not water.

This wouldn't be a problem, but there are multiple conversion factors, meaning you might get a *totally* different PPM reading simply because one meter uses a different conversion factor than another.

Because of this confusing terminology, I always recommend buying a meter that can display EC as well as TDS/PPM. That way you can get a "pure" reading of your nutrient concentration, and you can work from there.

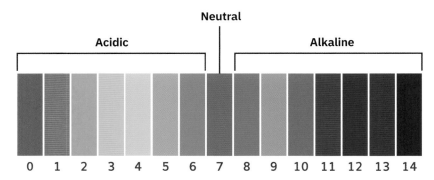

The pH sweet spot when growing hydroponically is between 5.5 and 6.5.

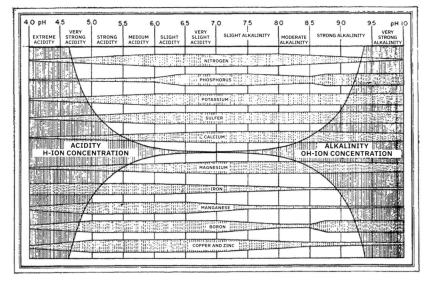

A representation of how plants uptake nutrients dependent on the pH of your water or soil.

pH

You might remember pH from your high school chemistry classes. It is a measure of how acid or basic a solution (or soil) is. It's measured on a scale from 1 to 14. A pH of 1 is considered an extremely acidic solution, and a pH of 14 is considered a highly basic solution. What does this have to do with water? Well, pure water is considered a 7.0 on the scale, otherwise known as *pH neutral.*

The optimal pH range for *most* plants is between 5.5 and 6.5. A pH in this range has a few advantages for us. First, a slightly acidic pH is an unfriendly environment for many of the waterborne algae species that can take over a hydroponic system. Second, your water needs to be in a certain pH range to avoid something called *nutrient lockout*, a condition where your plants cannot uptake the nutrients they need to survive and thrive.

Without knowing the basics of pH, you're likely to cause catastrophic problems for your hydroponic garden. Because you are forgoing the use of soil in hydroponics, it's crucial to keep a watchful eye on the pH of your nutrient solution.

NUTRIENT LOCKOUT

A pH that is too high or too low can completely shut down the ability of your plants' roots to uptake nutrients. This is bad; a well-balanced nutrient solution not only contains the right concentration of nutrients in relation to water, but the solution itself must also be within the correct range. Only then can you have a truly balanced nutrient reservoir.

The chart at left lists the most essential nutrients plants need for vigorous growth. Along with that list is a horizontal representation of the availability of each of these nutrients as you move along the pH scale. The thickness/thinness of each nutrient line represents the ability of a plant to absorb that particular nutrient at a specific pH level.

As you can see, plants find almost every nutrient hard to absorb at the far ends of the pH scale. However, you don't have to be too far off balance to hinder the growth of your plants. Take a look at pH 5.0. At that point, plants have trouble absorbing the three macronutrients as well as a handful of other nutrients. This is why maintaining a balanced pH is extremely important—small errors can hurt your plants. The "sweet spot" is generally considered to be around 6.2, although different plants require different pH levels.

Most liquid nutrients come with pH buffers. These ensure that your water is pH-corrected within the 5.5 to 6.5 range, which is really handy for hydroponic growers. However, this doesn't mean that you can completely forget about monitoring pH. As your plants grow, the pH will naturally fluctuate as the plants drink water and take up nutrients.

TESTING YOUR pH

To make sure your pH is always in the right range, pick up a simple pH meter. There are a few types I'd recommend, in order of cost:

- pH testing strips
- pH testing kit with solution
- digital pH meter

If you buy pH testing strips or a solution-based kit, you measure the pH by checking the color of your strip or solution against a reference chart. Typically, you're looking for an orangish or reddish color, which indicates your water is around the ideal range of 5.5 to 6.5. For the beginner hydroponic gardener, I recommend the strips or testing solution.

If you want to invest in a digital pH meter, your job will be easier—the meter will spit out an exact numerical reading of the pH based on the 1.0 to 14.0 scale. As long as you keep your meter calibrated and taken care of, it'll give you accurate readings for years to come.

The pH test strips are cheap but they can present an issue if (like me) you're partially color-blind.

As long as they're properly calibrated, digital pH meters make monitoring your nutrient solution a breeze.

Hydroponic Nutrients

Nutrients are the bedrock of your hydroponic system. Because you're growing in water and not soil, you need to manually add all of the macro- and micronutrients to your system.

The first thing to consider is the composition of your nutrients. Do they contain all of the elements your plants need? Are they in the right ratios? Secondly, what EC, or strength, should the nutrients be at for the plant you're growing, and where is it in its life cycle?

A complete hydroponic nutrient will have these elements present:
- nitrogen (N)
- phosphorus (P)
- potassium (K)
- calcium (Ca)
- magnesium (Mg)
- sulphur (S)
- iron (Fe)
- manganese (Mn)
- copper (Cu)
- zinc (Zn)
- molybdenum (Mo)
- boron (B)
- chlorine (Cl)

Depending on the company you buy your nutrients from, these elements will be present in different ratios. Most companies also make special blends for particular plants or stages of life. For example, General Hydroponics has a three-part series that's split into:
- **Grow**—heavier on nitrogen for vegetative growth
- **Bloom**—heavier on phosphorus and potassium for flowering and fruiting
- **Micro**—ensures plants get enough of the essential micronutrients they need

I recommend going with a simple liquid nutrient from a brand like General Hydroponics. Dry nutrients exist, but they're more complicated for a beginner grower to mix. You'll get by just fine with a liquid nutrient until you advance to expert level.

How to Prepare Your Nutrient Solution

Now that you understand how water and nutrients interact with one another in a hydroponic environment, you have to learn how to put these two ingredients together to form the perfect nutrient solution. This is extremely important because it's the bedrock of your plants' success in your system.

First, pour the purest source of water you have into a basin. Make note of the amount of water and use your conductivity meter to measure the amount of total dissolved solids in the water. If that's under 200 parts per million, you're usually in good shape. Above that, and you may need to use a hard water formulation of hydroponic nutrients.

What you need to prepare your nutrient solution: pH up, pH down, hydroponic nutrients, a digital pH meter, and water.

Add the micronutrient mixture first and stir well to avoid nutrients dropping out of solution.

If you're using a three-part nutrient, the order you add them to your water matters. Add micronutrients first, then vegetative nutrients, then bloom nutrients. Shake each container well before you pour into your measuring cup. Read the instructions on the back of the containers and add the amount suggested, taking care to wash your measuring cup between each nutrient.

Let the solution combine for a few minutes, then check the pH. If it's too high or too low, you'll need to add a pH adjusting solution. Pour either pH down or pH up into a small amount of water to dilute it; then add it to your nutrient solution.

General Hydroponics FloraMicro is being added to the water.

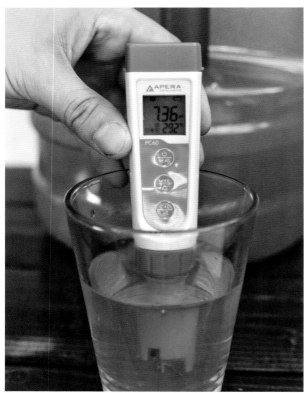

After adding all nutrients but *before* adjusting the pH, the solution is at a 7.36 pH, which is slightly too high.

After adding pH down, the solution is at 6.32 pH, which is the perfect range for most plants.

Tip: What Are pH Up and Down?

Commercial products can either raise or lower the pH of a nutrient solution. For example, pH down is typically food-grade phosphoric acid, though some gardeners use lemon juice; pH up is typically potassium hydroxide and potassium carbonate, though you can also use baking soda if you don't have access to commercial products.

Let the solution combine for ten to fifteen minutes, then check again and repeat until you have the correct pH (about 6.2).

As you become more familiar with your water and nutrients, you'll know exactly how to adjust your nutrient solution as time goes on. Take copious notes if you want to make the process easier the next time.

Hydroponic Growing Media

Hydroponics is soil-free, but that doesn't mean you don't need some material to support your plants. Although most of the work in hydroponics is done by your nutrient solution and grow lights, the growing medium provides a couple of advantages, such as:

- acts as support for your plant's roots, especially during the fragile seedling phase
- holds nutrients, water, and air to support plant roots

Following are some of the most common types of hydroponic growing media and the benefits of each. Don't be overwhelmed by the options; choose ones that are available in your area and to which you have easy access, and go from there.

Coco coir is one of my favorite products to use in my hydroponic systems.

Coconut Coir/Coco Peat

Coconut (coco) coir is quickly becoming a favorite among hydroponic gardeners. It's made from ground coconut husks and represents a giant leap forward in the sustainability of hydroponic growing media.

To understand why ground coconut husks are becoming so popular, let's take a look at what a coconut husk does for a coconut. Coconuts are grown in tropical regions, and oftentimes they fall into the ocean when they are ripe. The husk protects the seed and flesh from sun and salt damage. Most importantly, the husk acts as a great growing medium for the coconut to germinate and create new coconut trees.

Endlessly reusable, clay pellets cost a bit more up front but stand the test of time.

Now apply these benefits to hydroponics. The ground husks act as a great hormone-rich and fungus-free medium for your plants. Coir has a great air-to-water ratio, so you don't have to worry about drowning your roots. Best of all, it's completely renewable. Coconut husks would generally go to waste or be composted if they weren't used in hydroponic applications.

If you can't find coconut coir in your area, I recommend buying dehydrated and compressed coconut coir bricks online. It's much more economical to purchase them this way, meaning your money goes a long way.

Expanded Clay Pellets

Also known as *hydroton*, expanded clay pellets are one of the most popular types of growing media. As their name suggests, these are made by heating clay until it expands to form porous balls. These balls are inert and pH neutral. In addition, their spherical shape and porosity help ensure a good oxygen and water balance, so plant roots don't dry out or drown.

In my experience, the only two downsides to using hydroton pellets are their weight and their draining ability. In certain hydroponic systems, filling an entire system with expanded clay pellets is going to leave you with a very heavy system. They also drain and dry out very quickly because a lot of space remains between each pellet. However, they can be used to great effect to line the bottom of a growing tray when draining is an issue.

When you first purchase expanded clay pellets, be sure to rinse them a few times. The friction of transport can cause the balls to rub against one another and create clay dust, which you don't want clogging your system.

Be careful when working with perlite; wear a face mask to avoid breathing in particulates.

Rockwool is a staple in large-scale hydroponic food production.

Held together by a bioadhesive, starter plugs make life a whole lot easier in a hydroponic garden.

Perlite

You might recognize the word "perlite" from earlier chapters, as it's popular in soil gardening as well. It's created by heating volcanic glass to a point where it "puffs up" into an extremely light and porous material. It has one of the best oxygen-retention levels of all growing media because of its porosity.

It's not a good idea to use perlite by itself because its light weight can be a problem. It can shift around, wash away, or just float on top of the water. Growers typically mix perlite with coco coir or vermiculite.

Rockwool

Rockwool has been around for decades and is well known in the hydroponic growing community. It is made by melting rocks and spinning them at super-high speeds into extremely thin and long fibers, similar to fiberglass. These fibers can be pressed into cubes of varying sizes.

Rockwool has all of the benefits of most growing media—it's lightweight, holds water, and is inexpensive. It's quite often used to start seeds in a hydroponic system.

However, it has some interesting downsides. It's not easy to dispose of; those thin fibers of melted rock will last essentially forever. Additionally, they're usually of a too-high pH when purchased and need soaking in pH-balanced water before use. The fibers and dust created in the spinning and compressing process can be harmful to eyes, noses, and lungs. (You can prevent the dust by immediately soaking rockwool in water once you take it out of the package.)

Because of these downsides, rockwool is rapidly being replaced by peat- or coir-based starter plugs as a reliable medium for seed sprouting in your hydroponic garden.

Starter Plugs

A new and innovative entry into the hydroponic media space is what I call "starter plugs." These can be peat-, coir-, or compost-based, with the material bound together by a biodegradable adhesive.

If you're concerned about sustainability and organics, starter plugs are a great way to start seeds and incorporate them into your hydroponic system. I use these extensively for my seedlings and cuttings. They're the most convenient and simplest way to start large quantities of new plants.

All you have to do is place them in growing trays, sow your seeds, and provide the right environment for the seeds to germinate. Young roots will grow straight downward toward the opening at the bottom in the tray. This is helpful when transplanting into any type of hydroponic system because roots growing out to the sides aren't as beneficial.

If you don't have access to perlite, pumice can take its place.

Sand is available just about anywhere for the truly budget-conscious urban gardener.

Pet stores carry aquarium gravel at low cost and it makes an excellent hydroponic medium.

Pumice

Pumice is most similar to perlite in its advantage and disadvantages. It's a lightweight mineral that is crushed and used as structure for your plants' roots to grab on to. It's often quite cheap, making it a good budget option for a beginner hydroponic gardener.

Sand

Sand is one of the most plentiful types of growing media on the planet. It's extremely cheap (or free) and a great way to get started if you're low on funds. However, it's fairly heavy, must be sterilized often, and has poor water retention. Arguably the oldest hydroponic media, sand holds no water or nutrient load.

Because of these downsides, I recommend staying away from sand or at least mixing it with another growing media on the list that balances its weak points.

Gravel

Gravel is the same material used in most aquariums and makes a great growing medium as long as it is washed between use. It's relatively cheap and easy to clean. This is a great DIY starter media if you're short on cash.

One thing to watch out for with gravel is its propensity to cause swings in your pH levels if it is in contact with water.

Growing Under Artificial Lighting

I consider grow lights to be the most important purchase when it comes to an indoor garden. Without them, everything else you need to grow indoors successfully is quite literally worthless.

Most people think that grow lights are only used in very specific situations, but they have myriad uses for gardeners of all kinds. The most common reasons to grow under lights are these:

- Grow plants from start to finish in a hydroponic system.
- Start seeds in preparation for the growing season.
- Extend your growing season by bringing outdoor plants inside once the weather changes.
- Propagate and root cuttings.
- Grow plants harvested at a young age, such as baby greens, herbs, and microgreens.

Because there are so many different reasons to use grow lights, there are a lot of things to consider when it comes to buying, using, and caring for a light.

Before I go any further, it's helpful to understand a few basic concepts about light. Remember, when growing under artificial lighting, we are trying to mimic the sun; therefore, we have to get into a bit of the science of light.

Spectrum

All light, both visible and invisible, falls somewhere on a spectrum. This spectrum is measured in nanometers, which correspond to the wavelength of light. The particular band of the spectrum that we care about as indoor gardeners is the 400 to 735 nanometer range, also known as photosynthetically active radiation, or PAR.

As the name suggests, PAR refers to the wavelengths of light that plants can actually use for all of the processes related to photosynthesis. Within this band of light, there are subsections that plants use for specific purposes:

- **400** to **490 nanometers**— This "blue" light is used by plants primarily during their vegetative growth phase.
- **580** to **735 nanometers**— This "orange-red" light is used by plants during their flowering and fruiting phase.

Visible and Invisible Light

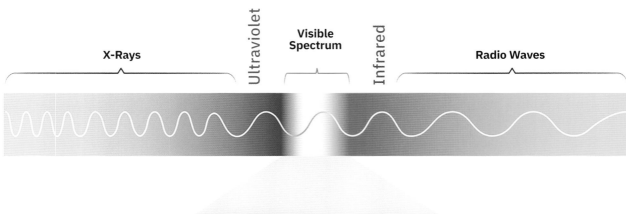

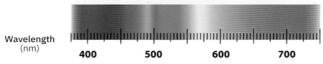

The full spectrum of light

You might be wondering, "What about the gap between 490 nm and 580 nm? Why don't plants use that range?" Surprise! They do. It used to be a common belief that plants were green because they didn't absorb light in the green spectrum. This isn't believed to be true anymore as most scientists agree that green light is useful in photosynthesis. That being said, plants still use less of green light than blue and red light.

Quantity

Now that we know the "type" of light (PAR) that plants need in order to grow, flower, and fruit, we need to figure out how much of that light they need. Here are a few acronyms to understand, then we'll translate into plain English.

- **PPF (Photosynthetic Photon Flux)**—How much light is emitted per second by a light source.
- **PPFD (Photosynthetic Photon Flux Density)**—How many photons are delivered per second over a meter squared, at a specific distance.
- **DLI (Daily Light Integral)**—How much light a particular plant needs to accumulate over a 24-hour period.

All of these are affected by the type of light you use, how powerful it is, and how far it is from your plants.

Footprint

The footprint of a grow light refers to how much surface area it covers. It's a function of the distance between your grow light and your plants.

The further your grow light is from your plants, the greater the footprint, but the lower the density of photons hitting your plants. The opposite is true if you place the grow light closer to your plants. Placing your grow lights correctly is a delicate balancing act among the heat output, the quantity of light, and the overall footprint of your light. Learning this comes with practice.

Photoperiod

Unlike growing outdoors, with indoor growing, you aren't limited by the amount of sunlight, so you can put your plants under lights 24/7 if you'd like. However, this usually isn't a good idea, as most plants have processes that *require* darkness as a trigger. Common lighting schedules for growing indoors are:

- **16/8**—This schedule is great for the vegetative phase of a plant's life, where it's putting out new growth and leaves.
- **12/12**—This schedule is great for the flowering and fruiting phases of a plant's life.

Types of Grow Lights

Now that we've covered some basic properties of lighting, let's get into the different types of grow lights on the market. This is a confusing topic for many gardeners due to all of the different technologies and the sometimes-misleading claims of lighting manufacturers.

I hope to shine some light (pun intended) on the different types so you can make an educated decision for your garden.

Inexpensive but energy-intensive metal halide bulbs are wonderful during a plant's vegetative phase of growth.

High pressure sodium grow lights tower over a hydroponic cucumber greenhouse.

METAL HALIDE (MH)

Metal halide grow lights are popular during the vegetative phase of a plant's life cycle. This is because they put out more light in the blue range of the spectrum. Plants use far more blue light in their vegetative phase than they do red light.

HIGH PRESSURE SODIUM (HPS)

High pressure sodium grow lights are used throughout a growing period, but they are especially favored during the flowering or fruiting phase. They put out a lot of red and orange light, which plants use heavily during the final stages of their lives.

Ceramic metal halide lights provide one of the broadest spectrums of light available in a single grow light.

A high-intensity T5 fluorescent shop light gives seedlings and young plants a head start on life.

CERAMIC METAL HALIDE (CMH)

Ceramic metal halide lights are some of the most exciting to come on the market. Although they sound like an offshoot of the classic metal halides, they actually work quite differently.

Growers are flocking to ceramic metal halide lights these days due to their balanced spectral output. They have a great mix of blue, orange, and red light. This makes them an excellent "all around" choice for growers.

Right now, they come in 315w and 630w sizes from a few different reputable manufacturers. The 315w systems typically replace a 400w HPS or MH light, so you're not only saving energy but also getting a better overall spectral output.

FLUORESCENT

Fluorescent lighting is extremely popular for the beginning stages of a plant's life cycle. Many hobby and commercial growers use them for starting seeds, rooting cuttings, and early to mid-stage vegetative growth.

They're extremely efficient from an energy standpoint, don't put out a lot of heat, and come in convenient sizes for indoor growers.

While it's possible to build your own setup with individual compact fluorescent lamp (CFL) bulbs, the standard these days is to use T5 fluorescent tubes in a variety of sizes. T8 and T12 bulbs also exist, but they're far less efficient and have fallen out of popularity.

When buying T5 lights, you have two decisions to make. One is, how many bulbs do you want? And the other is, how long do you want your fixture to be? The number of tubes in a fixture ranges from two to sixteen, and the length of fixtures ranges from 2 to 4 feet.

HIGH INTENSITY FLUORESCENT (HO/VHO)

There are two more varieties of fluorescent tubes. High output (HO) and very high output (VHO) use the same technology, but just put out more light.

Because they are more powerful, they also run hotter, so they must be placed farther away from your plant canopy to prevent burning.

LEDs are taking the hydroponic gardening world by storm due to their efficiency and low heat output.

LIGHT EMITTING DIODE (LED)

When LED grow lights first came on the market, they were met with a lot of skepticism for two reasons. First, manufacturers were making incredible claims about their effectiveness and efficiency. Second, they were a new lighting technology and old-school indoor growers were suspicious.

These days, LED lighting is more established and is very popular among some growers. LEDs have a few unique benefits that most other types of lights can't match.

First, they use a very low amount of energy and put out very little heat. This is a big factor for many growers who don't want to spend a lot of ongoing money to light their gardens and don't have the space to deal with a lot of heat output. They're also made up of many small diodes, meaning that each diode can be customized to put out a specific wavelength of light. The most advanced LED lights are custom-built by growers using chip on board (COB) LEDs for maximum light output and customizability.

Choosing the Right Grow Light

You've just taken in a lot of information about growing under lights. This table compares and contrasts the different lighting technologies as well as the features of each to allow you a quick way to select the light that's right for you.

Light	Wattage	Growing Area	Heat Output	Height from Plants
CFL	125	2 feet × 2 feet	Low	6 inches to 2 feet
2-foot T5 CFL, 4 bulbs	96	2 feet × 3 feet	Low	6 inches to 2 feet
4-foot T5 CFL, 4 bulbs	216	2½ feet × 5 feet	Low	6 inches to 3 feet
HPS	250	3 feet × 3 feet	Medium	2 to 3 feet
MH	250	3 feet × 3 feet	Medium	2 to 3 feet
HPS	400	5 feet × 5 feet	High	3 to 4 feet
MH	400	5 feet × 5 feet	High	3 to 4 feet
CMH	315	5 feet × 5 feet	High	3 to 4 feet
LED	180	2 feet × 4 feet	Low	1½ to 2 feet

Building Successful Hydroponic Systems

The beauty of hydroponics is in its flexibility. If you can imagine a system, chances are you can design it and build it. At the same time, that can be overwhelming. Fortunately, all hydroponic systems fall into about five categories, which I'll go over now.

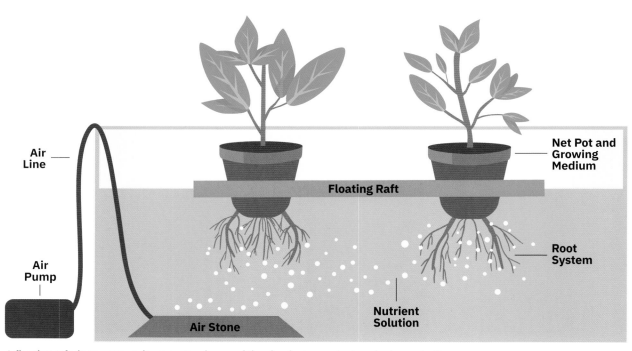

Deep Water Culture

Air Line

Air Pump

Air Stone

Floating Raft

Net Pot and Growing Medium

Root System

Nutrient Solution

A floating raft deep water culture system is one of the simplest ways to grow hydroponically.

Deep Water Culture

If you're new to growing plants hydroponically, words like "deep water culture" can sound like they're straight out of a science fiction movie. Don't fear—deep water culture is one of the simplest methods of hydroponic gardening out there.

WHAT IS DEEP WATER CULTURE (DWC)?

Before I get into the nitty-gritty details, let's get a high-level overview of this type of system. In a DWC system, a plant's roots are suspended in a well-oxygenated solution composed of water and nutrients. There are three critical parts of this solution:

- **Oxygen**—Because the roots are submerged in water and not soil (which has gaps and holes where air resides), the water needs to be well oxygenated so the plant doesn't drown. This is accomplished using an air pump and air stone.
- **Water**—Think of this system as if you're growing in soil and permanently watering your plants. This is one of the reasons growing hydroponically is so beneficial—you never need to "water" again.
- **Nutrients**—A good-quality soil contains all of the micro- and macronutrients that a plant needs to survive and thrive. Because we have no soil, we need to supplement the oxygen-rich water with nutrients so our plants can grow.

This method is called deep water culture for two reasons. First, you typically grow with a reservoir that can hold a decent amount of water. More water means more stability in your nutrient solution, which means less monitoring and maintenance for you. The second reason is because of how much of the rootball you submerge in the water. Other hydroponic methods expose root zones to air and drench them in water just a few times a day (ebb and flow systems are a good example of this). In deep water culture, most of your plant's root system is submerged 24/7, hence, the name.

BENEFITS OF DEEP WATER CULTURE

- low maintenance once it's set up
- extremely fast growing times compared to soil (I've grown lettuce to harvest in thirty days instead of sixty in soil)
- very few moving parts and assembly

DOWNSIDES OF DEEP WATER CULTURE

However, it's not all sunshine and roses. There are some issues with this type of system that can cause problems. These are mostly avoidable if you're maintaining your garden, though. The primary issues include these:

- in small systems, pH, water level, and nutrient concentration may fluctuate wildly
- roots are vulnerable to drowning if there is a power outage
- can be difficult to maintain a consistent water temperature

COMMON DEEP WATER CULTURE QUESTIONS (AND ANSWERS)

Should I use a singular or modular system?

If you're just starting out, go with a single reservoir setup. You can build them yourself or buy one of the many on the market. A modular DWC system is better for growers who know exactly what they want to grow and how much they want to grow. Start small and scale up as you get more experience.

Should my reservoir be sterile?

This is not a yes-or-no question. Some hydroponic gardeners want to keep their reservoir sterile. This means they won't have any of the biological contaminants that might plague a hydroponic garden, such as algae. But at the same time, they won't be able to take advantage of beneficial bacteria. If you decide to add beneficial bacteria to your reservoir, just be aware that it comes with the risk of having not-so-beneficial bacteria organisms tag along for the ride.

What should the temperature of my reservoir be?

This is one of the downsides of deep water culture; it can be hard to control the temperature of your reservoir. Aim for no higher than 68°F. If you get much higher, the oxygen level in your water starts to drop (even if you're oxygenating with an air pump and air stone).

Also try to keep it above 60°F. If it goes any lower, your plants think that they're moving into a new season, typically fall or winter. This means they'll start to divert more energy toward flowering, which you may not want.

How much of the roots should be submerged in my DWC reservoir and nutrient solution?

First of all, make sure that only the root matter is submerged in your nutrient solution—no stem and certainly no vegetation. You don't want to completely submerge the roots either. I personally keep about 1 to 1½ inches of roots above the water line. The bubbles from the air stone will typically pop, and water will still land on the roots that aren't submerged, so you don't have to worry about them drying out.

Are there any specific deep water culture issues to watch out for?

Monitor your garden for the following issues, all of which are common in DWC systems:

- root-related plant diseases such as pythium
- rapid fluctuations in pH or PPM/EC/TDS
- nutrient solution that is too warm

Deep Water Culture Herb Tote

This garden is designed to hold eight plants. If you want to expand it, feel free to do so; there's plenty of room to grow more herbs. Eight plants allow you to grow a lot of different types of herbs. Basil, sage, oregano, thyme, parsley, chives, tarragon, and cilantro are among the most popular herbs, but they aren't mandatory by any means.

Plant whatever you like in your garden, as long as it isn't an herb that grows to a massive size. The entire shopping list comes to around $50 to $80 or so, depending on where you get your materials.

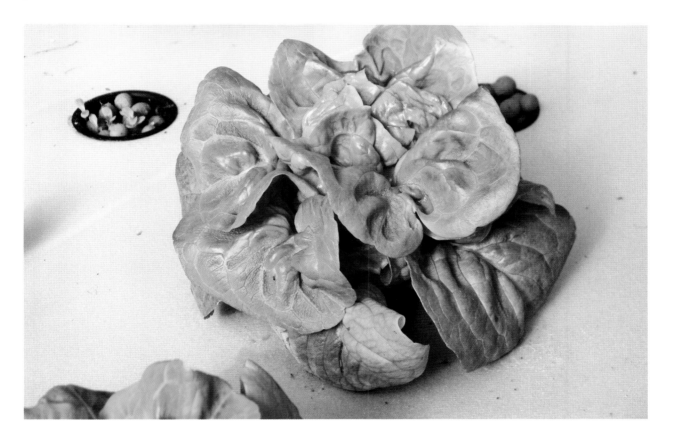

Materials

- 15-quart plastic tote
- 2-inch net pots (8 or more)
- permanent marker
- electrical tape
- spray paint
- drill
- 2-inch hole saw bit
- sandpaper
- ³⁄₁₆-inch drill bit
- ⅛-inch air line tubing
- air pump
- suction cups
- air stone
- pH testing kit
- pH down or up
- General Hydroponics FloraGro
- growing media
- seeds or starts

Steps

1. The tote needs to be perfectly clean before you paint. Make sure to wash and dry it completely to ensure a smooth, dry surface.

Once your tote is dry, take a net pot and place it parallel to the top of the tote. Make a mark on your tote at the bottom of the net pot; this is where your water line will be. Place a strip of electrical tape up to the mark you made on the tote.

2. You also need to spray paint your tote if it isn't already opaque to avoid algae buildup in the reservoir. Throw down some old newspaper or paper towels and place your tote on top. Make sure the top is fastened tight. Use broad strokes with a can of spray paint to cover the top and all of the sides, except for the bottom, with a light coat of paint.

After ten minutes, give each side a heavier coat. You want to make sure that as little light as possible penetrates the reservoir. Let it dry for forty-five minutes.

Once dry, remove the electrical tape. You now have a water line indicator so you can keep track of your nutrient solution without having to remove the lid.

3. After the paint dries, take your net pots and align them on the cover of your tote. Make sure that you space them evenly. I wanted to leave room to add an additional six net pots in my design, so you can definitely space yours out better if you are sticking with eight net pots. Mark their locations with a marker.

Once you're done with the layout, start drilling eight 2-inch circular holes into the cover in an X pattern. Be sure to sand off all of the extra bits of plastic so you have a nice, smooth set of holes with no debris.

Drill a hole slightly larger than your ⅛-inch air line tubing in the short side of your tote, just below the top edge. This will be the air line feed hole. It's important that this hole be drilled above your water line, or you'll have a constant leak and never be able to maintain adequate water levels in your reservoir.

4. Set up your air pump and plug it into the wall. Attach one end of your air line tubing to the pump and thread the other end through the hole you drilled, then plug it into the air stone. Affix the air stone to the bottom of the reservoir with suction cups.

If you bought a 15-quart tote, you'll need around 2½ gallons of water to fill the reservoir to the water indicator line. Regardless of how much water your reservoir requires, be sure to write it down. You'll need this number later when you add your nutrient solution.

Step 1

Make a mark on your tote at the bottom of the net pot.

Step 1

Cut a strip of electrical tape to the height of the mark you made on your tote.

Step 2

Make sure to coat multiple times to prevent light leakage.

Step 3

Net pots laid out over the top of the tote are used as a template before drilling.

Step 4

Air line tubing is threaded through the hole in the tote with an air stone attached to the bottom.

Step 6

Add some growing medium to the bottom of each pot, add your transplant, and then fill in around it.

5. Now that you have built your reservoir and filled it with water, you need to test the pH of the water and add nutrients. Most tap water is in the 7.0 to 8.0 range. The herbs you will be growing need water with a pH in the 6.0 to 6.5 range, so you will need to use some pH down.

Note that pH down is highly corrosive, so be sure not to get it on any part of your body. You don't need much to adjust the water; try a few drops to start. Mix it into the water thoroughly, and then test again.

It can take a while to get the pH just right; try not to get frustrated. This is one of the most important steps in making sure that your plants get all of the nutrients they require for vigorous growth. If you don't correctly adjust the pH, you

will prevent your plants' roots from absorbing certain nutrients.

Now you need to remember how much water you added to the reservoir. Take a look at the nutrient mixing chart on the back of your bottle of General Hydroponics FloraGro. This will give you the exact amount to mix into your system. If you're starting from seed or cuttings, use ¼ teaspoon per gallon, and if you're starting from established plants you've bought from a garden store, use 1 teaspoon per gallon.

In my example system I added 2½ gallons of water to the reservoir and bought some herb starts from the local home-improvement store, so I added 2½ teaspoons of nutrients to my reservoir.

We're almost done. On to the final step . . .

This eight-site herb growing machine is fully built and ready to grow.

6. Place the lid on the tote and drop the net pots into the holes. Now you need to add a bit of your growing medium to the bottom of each net pot. This will provide a little base support for the root structure once you plant your herbs.

If you're not starting from seed but decided to purchase some herb seedlings, then you'll need to wash away the dirt from their root systems. You want to start out with as clean a plant as possible to avoid any contamination in your reservoir.

Gently wash the dirt away from the roots, being careful to damage your plant as little as possible. When the roots are clean, you can go ahead and place it in your net pot.

If there are long roots that you can pull through the gaps in the net pot, go for it. This helps the root system reach the water sooner and flourish in the rich nutrient bath. If there are not long roots, that's okay; just cover the rest of the root system with your growing medium and plant the rest of your herbs.

7. Every day, check your plants' health and take a peek at the nutrient solution. You can even check the pH daily if you want to get a sense for how it fluctuates based on changes in the growing environment. I recommend changing the nutrient solution out fully once a week to avoid large changes in nutrient density or pH.

Ebb and Flow Systems

An ebb and flow system is just a different way to irrigate your plants hydroponically. In a typical setup, your plants will be in a tray in individual containers filled with a growing medium of your choice.

Unlike deep water culture, ebb and flow systems do not keep a plant's roots permanently suspended in a nutrient solution. Instead, a table is filled with the nutrient solution a fixed number of times per day, delivering the food and moisture to the root systems in specific doses. When the table is dry, the roots have a chance to absorb oxygen, ensuring that they don't drown.

While it's draining, the pump simply turns off and gravity draws the nutrient solution back down into the reservoir, which is an elegant solution.

BENEFITS TO EBB AND FLOW SYSTEMS

I consider deep water culture to be an even lower maintenance system than ebb and flow setups, but the ebb and flow method has some specific advantages. First, you can have a greater surface area to grow your plants by going the ebb and flow route. Because your reservoir is not directly connected to your plants, you can expand the size of your flood table. In DWC, your reservoir is also the container in which you grow your plants. So if you want a larger growing area, you have to enlarge your reservoir. Pretty soon you'll end up with an extremely heavy setup, which can be a real hassle.

It's also easier to control the temperature of your nutrient solution when it doesn't have to be in the same container as your plants. I've noticed that I have some trouble with DWC systems if I use them outdoors because the reservoir simply draws in too much heat from the sun. Pretty soon I've created an ideal growing environment for a lot of different pathogens and my plants' roots are absolutely hating me—not a recipe for growing success.

MAINTAINING AN EBB AND FLOW SYSTEM

To grow well in this system, you must plan and prepare accordingly. A simple irrigation timing error can wipe out your plants completely. On top of that, plants grow fast in an ebb and flow setup due to how efficient it is, so you have to monitor it constantly.

Ebb and Flow

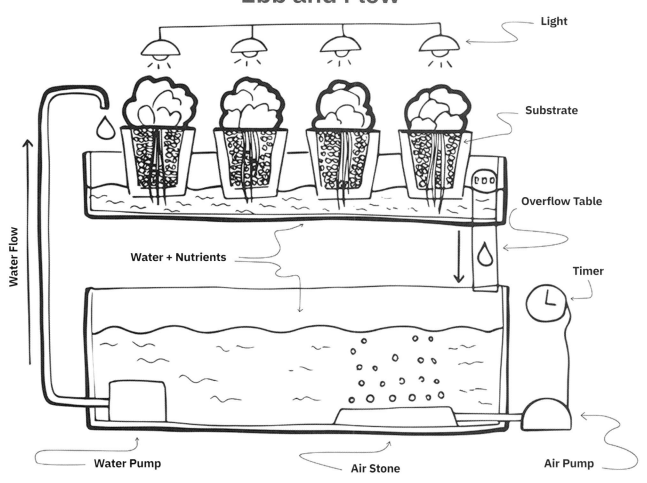

Light

Substrate

Overflow Table

Water Flow

Water + Nutrients

Timer

Water Pump

Air Stone

Air Pump

Ebb and flow systems make use of
gravity to drain the nutrient reservoir.

Compact Ebb and Flow Table

Ebb and flow is slightly more complex than deep water culture, but you should still be able to put this together with materials bought from stores in your area. For the flood and drain fittings, you *may* need to order from the Internet or visit a local garden center or hydroponics store.

In this system, you can grow larger plants such as tomatoes or peppers due to the system's larger size and modular design. It supports at least two different plants, although you can cram more in if you want a densely packed veggie garden.

These are the tools, fittings, tubing, and pumps you will need for this ebb and flow design.

Materials

- drill
- 1¼-inch hole saw
- 30-quart clear storage tote
- 16- to 20-gallon storage tote with lid
- fill and drain fitting set
- ½-inch black irrigation tubing, 18 inches (or more) long
- aquarium water pump, 120gph
- sissors
- air stone
- hydroponic nutrients
- 2 flowerpots
- hydroponic growing medium of your choice
- garden timer
- seedlings

These are the totes and pots you need for this design. I repurposed bed risers for the pots.

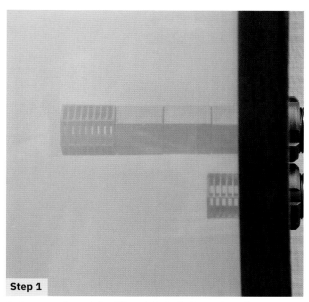

Step 1

A close-up view of the fill and drain fittings; the tall one is the overflow valve.

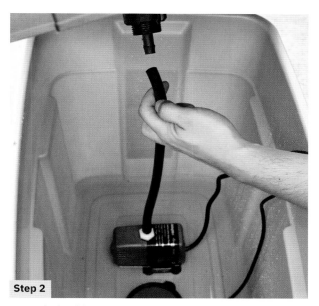

Step 2

Use ½-inch tubing to connect the water pump to the shorter fill and drain fitting.

Steps

1. Drill two 1¼-inch holes into the middle of the bottom of the clear storage tote. These will be where you affix your fill and drain fittings. Center the clear tote on top of the lid of the storage tote and drill matching holes exactly where you drilled them in the clear tote.

Drill one more 1¼-inch hole in the black lid, off to one of the corners. This hole is for the power plug of the water pump as well as the air line tubing.

Screw the fill and drain fittings to the center holes, taking care to put the rubber gaskets under the lid and tighten well.

2. Connect the ½-inch irrigation tube to the water pump, making sure it fits well. Trim it so it reaches the bottom of the shorter pipe fitting and slide the other end over it. Thread the pump power cord through the side port in the lid. You now have your pump line connected so nutrient solution can fill the top tote.

Now, place your air stone in the bottom of the tote next to the water pump. Run the air line tubing through the side port and snap the lid on top. Your water and aeration system is now in place, and you're ready to pH your water, add nutrients, and add your solution to the tote.

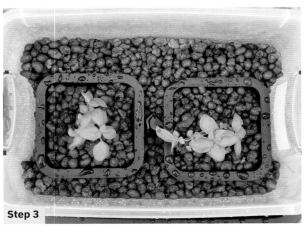

Step 3

A top-down look at the system, which is filled with expanded clay pellets and freshly transplanted basil.

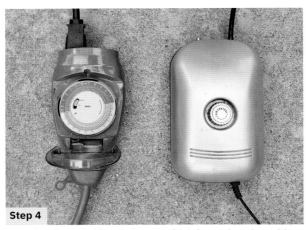

Step 4

A garden timer (left) and air pump (right) are placed outside the system.

3. Fill your reservoir with water and nutrients in the same method outlined at the beginning of this chapter. Pour it into the black tote and turn on your system to test it. Here's what should happen:

- Water should pump up into the top tote, filling it until it reaches the overflow fitting.
- Extra water should fall back down into the bottom tote, recycling itself.
- Air bubbles should be coming out of your air stone, oxygenating the solution.

At this point, all of the hard work is done. You have a functional ebb and flow system, but you're missing the pots and growing media you need to plant your seedlings. You can use almost any type of pot, but you have to make a few modifications.

Take your pots and drill drainage holes in the bottom and 1 inch above the bottom on each side to ensure they drain quickly once the pump timer turns off. Fill them up with a hydroponic medium or mix your own. For an ebb and flow system, a mixture I've found to work well is a 1:1 ratio of coconut coir and perlite, with some expanded clay pellets thrown in at the bottom to further improve drainage. Place the pots in the clear tote and add more clay pellets around them.

4. Your ebb and flow system is functional, but there are a few small tasks left. First, connect the garden timer to the pump so you can set a watering schedule. A classic ebb and flow schedule is four times per day for fifteen minutes each time. I usually set my times for 8 a.m., 12 p.m., 4 p.m., and 8 p.m. I don't flood the table at night.

Second, if you want to increase the oxygenation of your nutrient reservoir, you can add additional air stones and use the two to four outlet ports on most commonly available air pumps.

Now all that's left is to transplant your seedlings. When transplanting into this system, it's a good idea to water from the top for the first three to five days with some of your nutrient solution. This gives your fragile transplants time to establish themselves in their new home without drying out and dying.

Tips:
- Make sure you're growing on a level surface, otherwise your nutrient solution won't be evenly distributed.
- Avoid perlite-only as a growing medium, as it will cause containers to float.
- Adjust your irrigation schedule based on your climate and your plants' growth cycle.

The sit-on-top design of this ebb and flow system makes for a compact hydroponic garden.

Nutrient Film Technique (NFT)

The nutrient film technique, sometimes referred to as NFT, is one of the most popular types of hydroponic systems. It's prized for how versatile and modular it is. By adding more NFT channels to the system, you can significantly increase your yields without too much extra effort.

HOW NFT SYSTEMS WORK

NFT is very similar to the ebb and flow technique for one simple reason: They both use water pumps to deliver a nutrient solution to your plants.

In an NFT system, gravity ultimately guides the water back to the main reservoir. It's also a constantly flowing system as opposed to the flood and drain mechanics of an ebb and flow setup.

The key element of a good NFT system is how the nutrient solution flows over the roots. It has the word "film" in it for a reason—ideally, a very small amount of water flows through the channels. This allows your roots to get sufficient oxygen so they don't drown.

It's important to choose plants that don't need a lot of support when using an NFT setup. Lettuces, basil, and many other salad greens thrive in NFT systems, while fruiting plants such as tomatoes and cucumbers require much more support. It can still be done, but it's labor-intensive to set up the support structures for these types of plants.

BENEFITS OF NFT

Hydroponic gardeners use the nutrient film technique over other methods due to its low cost and maintenance requirements, as well as its flexibility. However, there are many other benefits to growing in an NFT system:

- low water and nutrient consumption
- avoids need to use a lot of growing media
- easy to disinfect roots and setup
- easy to see root quality and health
- consistent flow prevents salt buildup in root area
- recirculating, so minimal groundwater contamination
- modular and expandable

DOWNSIDES OF NFT

Every type of system has its disadvantages, and NFT is no exception. Because roots are growing in confined channels, they can clog the channels. More downsides include:

- failing pumps can kill an entire crop within a few hours
- does not work well with plants having large taproot systems
- does not work well with plants needing a lot of support

Nutrient Film Technique

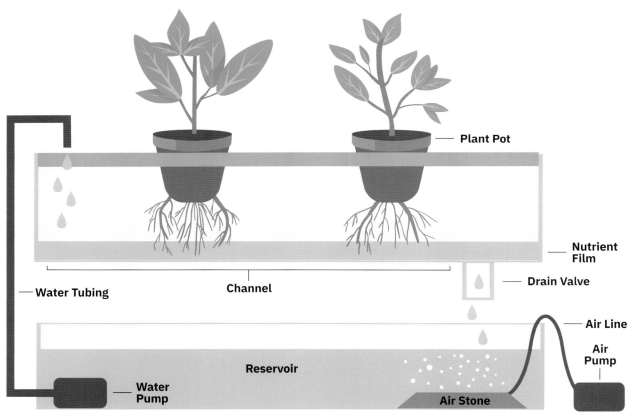

Plant Pot

Nutrient Film

Drain Valve

Air Line

Air Pump

Water Tubing

Channel

Reservoir

Air Stone

Water Pump

NFT systems use a thin layer of nutrient-enriched water to feed plants.

Growing Tips for Your Nutrient Film Technique System

Control your environment.
This isn't a tip that is specific to NFT; you should always control your environment to the best of your ability. It's important in NFT systems in particular because plant roots are more exposed than with other methods. This makes controlling air temperature, humidity, and airflow even more important.

Decide how to start your plants.
How you start your plants determines their future success in your NFT system. It's common to start in rockwool cubes, but I personally prefer to use peat- or coconut- coir-based starter plugs. However you decide to start seeds, make sure they're easy to transplant into your system.

Transplant into your NFT system at the right time.
Make sure that you transplant your plants into your system when the roots have developed to the point where they're already peeking out of the starter plug (or whatever else you used to start seeds). By waiting until this point, you're allowing the roots to have immediate access to water and nutrients once they're in the system.

Keep your nutrient solution calibrated.
You'll find your plants thriving in your NFT system compared to other methods, and doubly so compared to soil. But that increased growth means increased water and nutrient uptake. Make sure your plants are using water and nutrients at the same rate. If they're not, top up one or the other (or both) appropriately.

Remember to change your reservoir.
About every week it's a good idea to change out your reservoir completely. The larger your tank, the longer you can go without a complete nutrient solution change, but it's better to change more often than wait too long. This ensures a perfectly calibrated system with the right amount of nutrition for your growing plants.

Keep light out of your reservoir and channels.
Make your life easier by keeping your roots in the dark. If light gets through and hits the roots and nutrient solution, you are opening yourself up to algae growth, which is both a pain to deal with and affects the growth rate of your plants.

Keep your environment clean.
This is a no-brainer. Everything around your NFT system should be as clean as the system itself. When you harvest from the system, give it a deep cleaning before you transplant new seedlings in.

Start slow.
After you transplant your seedlings into your system, don't go too strong with the nutrient solution. The recommendations on the labeling of most hydroponic nutrients is higher than your seedlings need, so cut it by 25 to 50 percent, gradually moving up as your plants develop.

Use a half-strength nutrient solution to start your plants off, moving to two-thirds, and then to full dosage rate (as detailed on the bottle) after the first nutrient solution change (about seven to ten days after planting).

Check your root health.
Peek into your NFT channels once in a while to monitor your root health. They should be bright white and flourishing.

Sit-on-Top NFT Channel System

This system is a fantastic way to get started with the nutrient film technique and perfect if you'd like to dip your toes into the pond of hydroponics without going absolutely crazy. It uses PVC pipe as the NFT channel and gravity to feed the nutrient solution back into the main reservoir. As with all of these plans, it's easily customizable and extendable to your unique growing space.

Step 1

Be sure to evenly space each hole to give your plants ample room to grow.

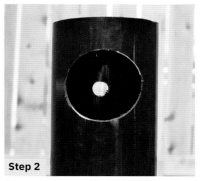

Step 2

At one end of your PVC pipe, drill a hole in the bottom for water to drain back into the system below.

This NFT design is compact, aesthetically pleasing, and quite productive once you get growing.

Materials

- saw
- 4-inch PVC pipe, 3-feet long
- drill
- 3-inch hole saw drill bit
- ¾-inch drill bit
- two 5-inch PVC flat caps
- two 2×4 lumber, 1-foot long each
- 25-gallon storage tote
- 1-inch hole saw drill bit
- submersible water pump, 75 gph
- 6 feet of ¾-inch black vinyl tubing
- hydroponic nutrient solution
- three 3-inch net pots
- expanded clay pellets
- seedlings

Steps

1. For simplicity's sake, this system is designed with the channel sitting right on top of the storage tote. Cut your 4-inch PVC pipe to size, making sure it fits into the tote lengthwise with a little room on either end so that the water can run back into the tote to recirculate.

Drill 3-inch holes into the PVC pipe, evenly spaced. These are where you'll drop your net pots when it comes time to plant.

2. On the opposite side of the PVC, drill a ¾-inch hole directly below one of the 3-inch holes. This hole will allow your water to drain back into the tote below.

Step 3

Make sure you drill this hole on the *opposite* side you drilled your drainage hole.

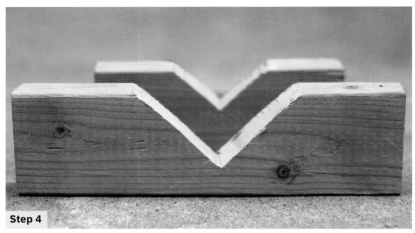

Step 4

Make sure one of your notches is 1 inch deeper than the other so water will drain in the correct direction.

Step 6

Vinyl tubing on the left is for drainage and to the right is for pumping into the NFT channel.

3. Take one of your PVC caps and drill a ¾-inch hole into the middle. This hole is where you'll connect your waterline so you can irrigate your channel.

4. Last, take your 2×4 lumber and cut a notch in each to support the channel. For optimal water flow, the channel should slope at a 1:30 ratio, meaning that if your channel is 30 inches long, it should have a vertical drop of 1 inch. Make sure the support with the larger notch cut out of it is on the same side as the ¾-inch drainage hole you drilled into your PVC pipe.

5. Drill a ¾-inch hole in the lid of the storage tote to complete the drainage section of this system. Drill a 1-inch hole in the lid to feed the power cord for the water pump through. Place your water pump in the bottom of the storage tote.

I'm using my go-to expanded clay pellets as the growing medium with transplanted basil.

6. Cut a 4-foot section of black vinyl tubing, fitting one end to the water pump and the other end through the PVC cap. Cut another 10-inch section of tubing and fit it through both ¾-inch holes in the channel and the top of the lid. Place your support on top of the lid and place the channel on the supports.

Fill your reservoir with properly prepared nutrient solution (referring to the guidelines earlier in this chapter). Add your net pots and expand clay pellets, and transplant your seedlings. Plug in the water pump and make sure that water is pumping up into the channel and draining back into the storage tote, completing the recirculating cycle. Your pump should be constantly be turned on.

Aeroponics

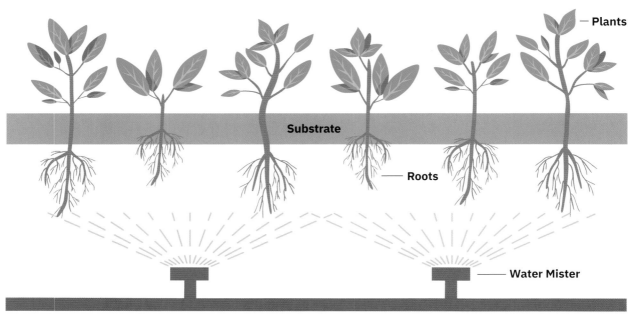

Plants

Substrate

Roots

Water Mister

Aeroponics exposes a plant's roots to the most air out of all of the hydroponic methods available.

Water Line

Aeroponics

Aeroponic systems are some of the most "high-tech" hydroponic setups that you can build. But they're not that complex once you understand how they work.

An aeroponic system is similar to an NFT system in that the roots are mostly suspended in air. The difference is that an aeroponic system achieves this by misting the root zone with a nutrient solution constantly instead of running a thin film of nutrient solution along a channel.

Some gardeners prefer to mist on a cycle like an ebb and flow system, but the cycle is much shorter, typically only a few minutes between each misting. It's also possible to mist on a continual basis and use a finer sprayer to ensure more oxygen gets to the root zones.

Aeroponic systems have been shown to grow plants even quicker than some of the simpler systems like deep water culture, but this has not been verified to be true in all cases. If you want to experiment with this system, you will need specialized spray nozzles to atomize the nutrient solution, or you can use sprinkler heads to approximate the effect.

This is an example of a commercial-scale aeroponics system. Inside the structure, sprayers are misting the roots of these trays of lettuce.

Aeroponic Bucket System

This 5-gallon aeroponic bucket system is practically identical to a design for a deep water culture system, except for the plumbing. It's lightweight, easily moved, and one of the simpler hydroponic systems to put together.

I love using systems like this aeroponic bucket as a plant cloning and propagation station.

Steps

1. Lay your net pots out on top of the bucket. If you want to grow one large plant, use a single net pot in the center of the lid. If you want to grow multiple small plants, you can use up to seven 3-inch net pots with this system. Trace around the circumference of each net pot with your permanent marker.

Drill your holes and check to see how the net pots fit. They should be snug and the lip of the net pot should hug the surface of the lid.

2. Place your pump in the bottom of the bucket and screw your 12-inch cut-off riser to it. Cut it to the height you want your sprayer to be, then attach the 360-degree sprinkler head. Run the power plug out of the top of the lid and plug it into your garden timer on repeating thirty-minute intervals, or just leave it on 24/7.

3. Fill your bucket with prepared hydroponic nutrient solution and place the lid on top. To plant into this system, I recommend using seed starting plugs with transplants, and filling the rest of the net pot with coconut coir or expanded clay pellets for additional support.

4. You don't need to worry about watering from the top when you transplant into the system. The 360-degree sprinkler head will wet the bottom of the net pots, bringing moisture right to the root zone.

Materials

- 3-inch net pots, up to 7
- 5-gallon bucket with lid
- permanent marker
- drill
- 3-inch hole saw bit
- submersible water pump
- ½-inch × 12-inch cut-off riser
- saw
- ½-inch 360-degree sprinkler head
- garden timer
- hydroponic nutrient solution
- seed starting plugs
- transplants
- coconut coir or expanded clay pellets

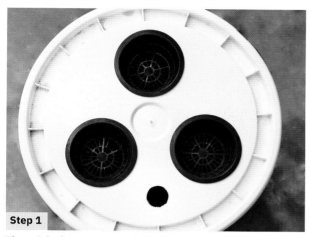

Step 1

Three 3-inch net pots are sitting in the lid with an additional hole for the water pump cord.

Step 2

The spray pattern of a 360-degree sprinkler head.

Step 2

You can use specialized sprayers if you want, but sprinkler heads at a local hardware store will do just fine.

Step 3

This 5-gallon bucket design is one of my favorite portable hydroponic systems.

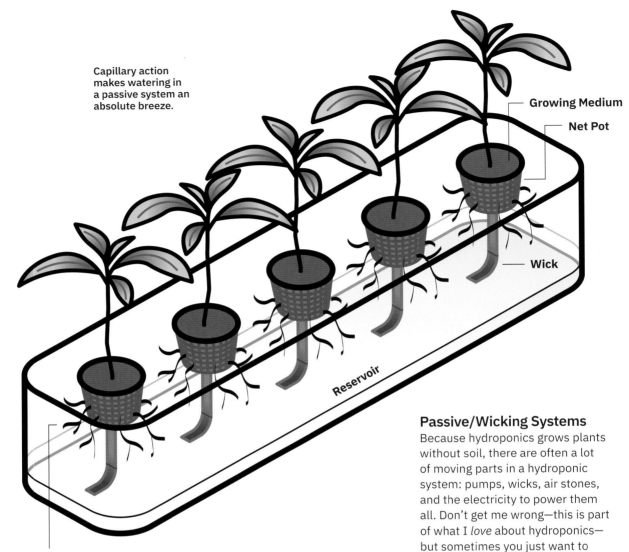

Capillary action makes watering in a passive system an absolute breeze.

Growing Medium

Net Pot

Wick

Reservoir

Roots "grow into" the nutrient reservoir.

Passive/Wicking Systems

Because hydroponics grows plants without soil, there are often a lot of moving parts in a hydroponic system: pumps, wicks, air stones, and the electricity to power them all. Don't get me wrong—this is part of what I *love* about hydroponics—but sometimes you just want to keep it simple.

This is where a passive system shines. It's a technique that allows you to grow hydroponically without electricity, pumps, or wicks of any kind. In fact, you don't even have to change your reservoir or add nutrients. It's as close to a completely "hands-off" growing technique as I've ever seen.

In a traditional deep water culture setup, you typically have your plant in a net pot with growing medium and you place it in a reservoir. Then you fill the reservoir with nutrient solution up to a certain point, making sure it doesn't touch the net pot.

The air stone that you add to your system will create bubbles that pop at the surface of the water, hitting your growing media and feeding your plant's young root system. As the roots grow, they'll eventually hit the surface of the water and growth will explode from there on out.

With a passive system, you fill your reservoir with nutrient solution, making sure to cover the bottom third of the net pot with water. The reason? Without an air stone, your plants will need water at the start of their lives, and this technique ensures they'll never dry out because your growing media is constantly wet.

As the plant continues to grow, it will use water and the water level will decline, but your plant's roots will have descended into the nutrient solution by that time.

You might be wondering, "Aren't air stones used for more than just wetting the growing media in the seedling phase?" You're right—this is where the beauty of passive hydroponics starts to shine. Because you are not refilling your reservoir, your plants will keep using up water and exposing more and more of their root systems to the air, which will ensure your plants get enough oxygen to survive and thrive.

There are a few considerations to take into account before you get started with a passive system.

Wicking systems can be either soil or hydroponics, depending on your personal preference.

BEST FOR LEAFY GREENS

This is designed to be a simple, hands-off method. That means it can't really account for the increased nutrient and water requirements of plants that bear fruit. Use this for leafy greens such as lettuces, spinach, and so on—not fruiting plants such as tomatoes or cucumbers.

PESTS

Because your nutrient solution will be still (because you're not using an air stone), it can draw the attention of pests, namely mosquitoes. To avoid this, make sure that the reservoir is protected from any type of bug or pest, while allowing some oxygen and air to flow in as well.

WATER QUALITY

You are not going to be replacing or adjusting the water level in your reservoir, so it's important to start with very high-quality water. I recommend reverse osmosis or filtered water; get your PPM as low as possible so you avoid a dangerous concentration of salts.

WATCH YOUR pH

If you're new to the method, you may want to pick up a pH pen and test the water every day. Once you get the hang of how to prepare your nutrient reservoir for the plant that you're growing, you can leave the system to do its job.

Adding frozen bottles of water to your reservoir can drop the temperature 5°F during the hottest parts of the day.

Keeping Your Hydroponic Reservoir Cool

One of the more annoying problems you'll run into as a hydroponic gardener is keeping your nutrient reservoir cool. A cool reservoir is crucial to squeeze as much yield out of your plants as possible and to minimize disease.

Hydroponic nutrient reservoirs tend to heat up quickly, whether you're growing indoors under lights or outside in the bright sun. This bumps up the temperature of the nutrient reservoir, which increases the temperature around the root zone. Because of this, the amount of dissolved oxygen in the root zone is lowered. When you combine these factors with the fact that plants grow faster in a hydroponic environment, you've created the perfect storm for oxygen deprivation. And when that happens, your plants are at risk of infection by pathogens such as pythium.

For best results, you want your air temperature to be higher than your water temperature. Typical ranges are 75° to 80°F for air temperature, and 68°F or lower for water temperature.

SO HOW DO I COOL MY HYDROPONIC RESERVOIR?

There are a number of ways you can cool down your reservoir ranging both in price and how annoying they are to deal with on a daily basis.

Regardless of the method you choose, make sure to ramp up your cooling efforts in the warm summer months, *especially* if you use a deep water culture or small-reservoir system (the small reservoir size heats up faster).

Paint Your Reservoir

If you have a clear reservoir, you'll want to spray paint it to block out light and prevent algae growth. When painting your reservoir, remember that darker colors will block out more light, but also absorb more heat. Lighter colors will block out less light and absorb less heat. I usually opt for a light grey color to get the best of both worlds.

Keep It in the Shade

This is a really obvious tip, but I feel like I had to mention it. If you can minimize the amount of light hitting the reservoir itself, you'll be minimizing the amount of heat that is transferred to your nutrient solution. Keep it in a shady area or cover the surface with cardboard or aluminum foil.

Increase the Size of Your Reservoir

Many hobby hydroponic growers use smaller reservoirs, which are prone to swings in water temperature. By building or buying a larger nutrient reservoir, you can add some stability to your temperature without building or buying any other cooling materials. As an added bonus, your pH and PPM will remain more stable as well due to the larger volume of water.

This Mason jar is spray-painted white to prevent light from heating the water.

Top Off Your Solution

An elegant solution is to simply add cooler nutrient solution to balance out the temperature in the reservoir. This isn't a solution you can use all of the time, because chances are high that if you have a temperature issue, it's a persistent one. Use this suggestion as a spot-fix if you have a onetime temperature fluctuation.

Be careful, though. If you add cooler nutrient solution quickly, the drastic temperature change could shock your roots.

Bury Your Reservoir in the Ground

If you're growing outside, you can dig out the ground and bury your reservoir. The cool, dark environment below the surface of the soil will keep the reservoir exceptionally cool. You'll almost never go into danger zone temperatures in the root zone if you use this method—but it does require a lot of effort.

Make a Swamp Cooler

A swamp cooler is a pretty ingenious cooling method; I didn't know about it until I did some research. If you take a simple clip-on fan and blow it across the top of the reservoir, you will see incredible temperature drops. You can expect a 5° to 10°F decrease in temperature—but at a cost.

Usually you'll need to top up your reservoir more often, because swamp coolers are utilizing evaporative cooling (meaning you're losing water to the air). If you think about this deeper, this also means that your PPM will increase due to evaporation, so keep a watchful eye on your measurements if you use this technique.

Buy a Chiller

The most effective (and most expensive) method is to buy a water chiller. These are electric units similar to air-conditioning units that are made for operating under water. They're basically composed of fans, compressor coils, and a refrigeration line.

All you do is plug and play with these bad boys. To cool your reservoir even more quickly, make sure you're circulating the water around. Most hydroponic gardeners will use a 1.5 to 2 horsepower chiller to handle most of the cooling responsibilities and then manage the rest on a case-by-case basis.

8

Growing Problems

No matter how experienced you are with plants, you're going to run into some issues throughout your growing journey. Whether it's a pest infestation, disease, or a simple watering issue, this chapter is designed to cover the most common growing problems and their solutions.

In this chapter, you'll learn how to:
- **Organically combat the most common bugs**
- **Deal with pesky animals munching on your crops**
- **Prevent and control the six most common plant diseases**

Colorado beetles are devouring these tender potato leaves.

Pests

Ah, pests. They are the bane of every gardener's existence. There's nothing like spending months growing gorgeous heirloom tomatoes only to wake up one day and see massive holes in the leaves and stems courtesy of the tomato hornworm. Or walking out into the garden one morning and having your heart sink as you see a gopher decimating your carefully tended-to veggie garden.

While your garden will never be 100 percent pest-free, this chapter will give you an understanding of how to troubleshoot common pest issues, strategies that work for almost all pests, as well as specific prevention and control guides for the nastiest ones you'll run into in the garden. It's also important to note that the local ecosystem you build by starting a garden requires some pests, because beneficial, predatory, and parasitic insects feed on them (and do a lot of your pest control work for you). So don't freak out if you have a little pest issue.

General Rules for Pest Prevention

KEEP PLANTS HEALTHY

Cultivating strong, healthy plants is a fantastic first step to preventing pests. Healthy plants aren't guaranteed to be pest-free, but they're much better suited to fighting off small infestations and recovering. If your plants are stressed for some reason, it's much easier for pests to take over. It's the same as when you're tired, overworked, or underfed; you get sick much more easily.

DAILY MONITORING

As the saying goes, an ounce of prevention is worth a pound of cure. Make inspecting your crops for pest damage a part of your daily gardening routine, and you'll be much more successful in the garden. Oftentimes you'll see clusters of eggs that you can brush off with your finger or squish, killing off the next generation of that pest and reducing its numbers.

If the problem is already severe, daily inspections help cut down on the chances that your plants will be absolutely decimated.

PHYSICAL BARRIERS

Sometimes, you have to take a more active role in pest prevention, and there's no better way to do this than by erecting physical barriers around your precious plants. For insects that mature into flying adults, row covers are a surefire way to protect your plants.

Row covers are my number one recommendation for physical pest prevention.

Mature adults won't be able to land on the leaves of your plants and lay their eggs, meaning they can't continue their life cycle. While this method doesn't guarantee you'll prevent all of the pests (they can always land somewhere that's unprotected), it does guarantee that the plants you have under cover will be safe.

I like to use row covers or protection on my *Brassica* crops (such as kale, broccoli, cauliflower, and so on) because in my experience, they're the most pest-prone plants I grow.

CROP ROTATION

When you hear the words "crop rotation" you probably think of a large-scale industrial farming technique. But it's useful in small gardens as well, especially when growing in raised beds. Some pests, like the aptly named cabbage moths, only prefer certain types of plants. If you've been ravaged by one of these territorial pests, rotating where you plant a susceptible crop the next season can reduce the number of pests you get in that area. Crop rotation is also an extremely useful strategy for soilborne pests such as root knot nematodes.

THREE-STAGE LIFE CYCLE

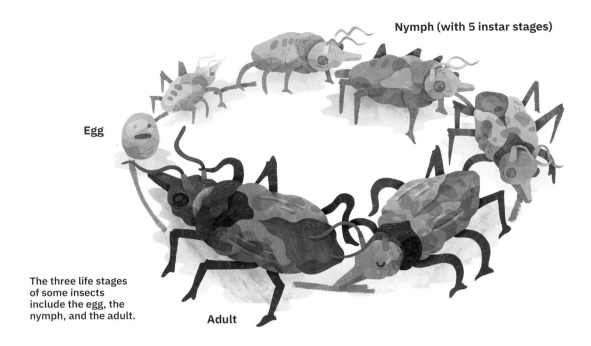

Nymph (with 5 instar stages)

Egg

The three life stages of some insects include the egg, the nymph, and the adult.

Adult

Insects

Bugs are easily the most destructive type of pest you'll find in your garden. Whether it's a huge caterpillar such as a tomato hornworm or a barely visible spider mite, bugs can wreak havoc on your plants in a short amount of time.

Before I get into descriptions of specific bugs, it's vital to understand the life cycle of most insects. Most insects go through three or four stages as they develop. Different bugs attack your plants at different stages of life. If you can disrupt a pest's life cycle, you have a good chance of eradicating it completely. After all, if none of them can reproduce, there won't be any left.

Eggs come in all shapes and sizes, and each pest has its own preference for where it likes to lay its eggs. Some prefer the undersides of leaves; some prefer the base of a stem. Regardless, the egg stage is the easiest one to combat. All you have to do is wipe the eggs off your plants and you're preventing the next generation of the pest from being born.

The **nymph stage** is a feature of insects with a three-stage life cycle and looks very much like the adult forms of these pests. The stages are called "instars," and the number of instars that occur before an insect reaches its adult form depends on the pest. Because insect nymphs typically hang out in the same habitat as their adult counterparts, the prevention and control techniques are similar to those for adults.

The **larval stage**, a feature of insects with a four-stage life cycle, is probably the most diverse stage of life. The larvae of pests typically hang out on your plants and start munching away, gathering enough energy to move on to the next stage of life. It's important to know that beneficial insects also go through the larval stages, like the classic ladybug/ladybird. Ladybug larvae look *far* different from adult ladybugs and are often mistaken for a pest, when this couldn't be further from the truth. They go straight for the eggs and young larvae of pests in your garden.

FOUR-STAGE LIFE CYCLE

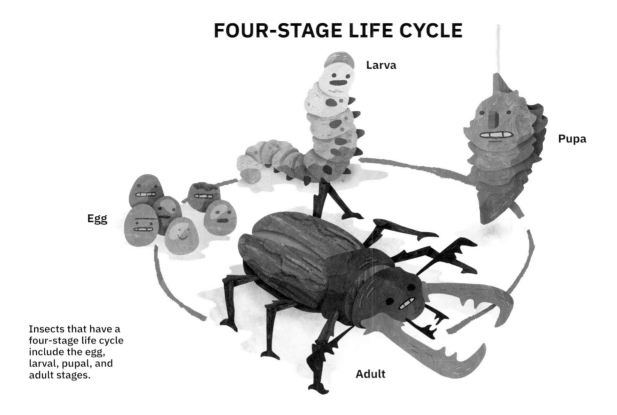

Larva

Pupa

Egg

Adult

Insects that have a four-stage life cycle include the egg, larval, pupal, and adult stages.

The **pupal stage** is the next stage for larvae, where they undergo the transformation to their adult form. They are at their most vulnerable in this form because they are stationary for long periods of time. However, they're also harder to find, as many insects burrow into the ground when they enter this stage.

Once insects reach their **adult stage**, it's time for them to reproduce. They often have increased mobility, either flying or crawling around to new areas of your garden. The adult stage is often the hardest stage for gardeners to combat due to how hard flying pests can be to capture. Using floating row covers, sticky traps, and organic sprays are all good options in this stage.

Brown marmorated stink bug eggs are visible on this weeping fig tree leaf.

Aphids are the bane of every urban gardener's existence.

TOMATO HORNWORMS

Anyone who's as much a fan of homegrown tomatoes as I am is terrified of this fat green tomato worm, and for good reason. Tomato hornworms can destroy tomato plants in rapid-fire fashion. But there's hope. With some preparation and careful management, you can get rid of this garden pest and keep it from coming back.

Tomato hornworms are some of the biggest caterpillars you're likely to find in your garden. On average, these tomato worms are 3 to 4 inches in length. They are bright green with around seven diagonal V shapes along their sides. A black tail-like horn protrudes from the rear.

A close relative, the tobacco hornworm, has a red-colored horn and diagonal white stripes instead of V shapes, but it is otherwise identical. Both tomato and tobacco hornworms prey on similar plants, so it's quite possible to misidentify one as the other because they do the same types of damage.

Hornworm Prevention

- Grow your plants under row covers.
- Sprinkle diatomaceous earth on your plants and surrounding soil as a deterrent.
- Till your garden at the end of the season to dig up overwintering insect populations, leaving the surface open for birds.

Organic Tomato Hornworm Controls

- Inspect susceptible plants daily and handpick these large bugs.
- Release lacewings and ladybugs, both of which eat the eggs of the tomato hornworm.
- Use a *Bacillus thuringiensi* (Bt) spray to kill existing hornworms.

APHIDS

There are over 4,400 species of aphids, of which approximately 250 are destructive in your garden. They come in all colors: black, white, green, reddish, pinkish, brownish, and more. They suck the sap out of your plants' leaves, and your plants die.

Sounds intimidating, right? It shouldn't be. No matter what species, all aphids have similar life cycles and all can be defeated in the same way.

Most aphids are pear-shaped with long antennae and long legs. Adult aphids usually have no wings, but some species do have winged forms. You'll often find them on the undersides of your plants' leaves where they suck the sap from them. They're not easily removed, even if you shake or brush the plant.

Aphid Prevention

- Dust susceptible plants with diatomaceous earth.
- Spray your plants with neem oil.
- Grow your plants under row covers.

Organic Aphid Controls

- Insecticidal soaps will kill these soft-bodied insects.
- For hardier plants, you can spray the plants with water and knock aphids off.
- Release ladybugs in your garden as they decimate aphid populations (by eating them!).

Despite their large size, tomato hornworm caterpillars can be deceptively hard to detect.

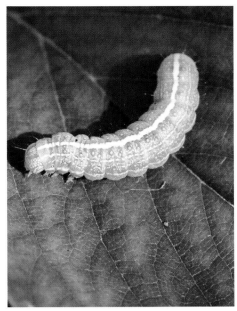

The pest I have to deal with the most in my own personal garden, cabbage worms will make short work of your *Brassicas*.

CABBAGE WORMS

You're starting to find holes in the leaves of your kale, and for that matter, in your cabbage, brussels sprouts, or other *Brassica*-family plants. The leaves of the neat rows of radishes you've planted are showing signs of chewing, too. Some leaves have little off-white or yellowish spots on their undersides. And you just saw a little green worm wandering over a leaf on your produce.

I'm sorry to be the bearer of bad news, but you probably have cabbage worms (*Pieris rapae* or *Pieris brassicae*).

There are two major species you'll see in the garden, the small cabbage moth and the large cabbage moth. Both look similar in their adult form: they're white butterflies with a black dot on their wings. They lay their small, green eggs on the underside of your plants. These eggs will either be singles or in clusters depending on the type of cabbage worm.

Cabbage Worm Prevention

- Use garlic spray to discourage the adult butterflies from laying eggs on your plants.
- Grind up citrus rinds in water. and spray your plants with it.
- Spray neem oil on the underside of leaves to smother eggs.

Organic Cabbage Worm Controls

- On a daily basis, scan the undersides of leaves; squish any cabbage worm eggs between your fingertips.
- Use BT spray on cabbage worm larvae to kill them quickly.
- Use a spinosad or pyrethrin-based spray.
- Dust your plants and surrounding soil with diatomaceous earth as a deterrent.

Although they're beautiful, these metallic bugs will munch away at your leaves.

Fungus gnats are exceptionally prevalent indoors, so keep an eye out.

JAPANESE BEETLES

A common culprit in the garden is the Japanese beetle. Although the insect is only ½ inch in length, it can do a lot of damage to flowers and vegetables because it usually feeds in groups. It doesn't help that these beetles aren't picky eaters; they can and will invade and consume more than 300 species of plants.

It's easy to identify this beetle by its distinctive appearance. It has a copper-colored back, a metallic blue-green head, and small white hairs that line the sides of its abdomen. These insects have six legs, two antennae, and wings.

Japanese Beetle Prevention
- Use homemade spray to bait Japanese beetle grubs (their larval form) up to the surface.
- Liquid dishwashing soap mixed with water should lure them to the surface of the soil, where they're vulnerable to birds.
- Introduce milky spore *Paenibacillus pappilae* to the soil, where the grubs will ingest it and die.

Organic Japanese Beetle Controls
- Handpick the large adult beetles from your plants and drop them into soapy water.
- Grow under row covers to prevent adults from laying eggs.
- Use traps designed specifically for Japanese beetles.
- Lay a sheet of fabric on the ground to lure beetles. In the morning, shake them into a bucket of soapy water.

FUNGUS GNATS

One of the most frustrating pests in many indoor gardens is the dreaded fungus gnat and its young, the fungus gnat larvae. These little buggers can absolutely destroy your plants if you're not vigilant—and they can do it quickly.

The primary way that fungus gnats affect your plants is through their larvae. They lay eggs in your growing medium. Once they hatch, the larvae will attach to the roots of your plants and drain them of nutrients.

Although the larvae are the main negative actors, adult fungus gnats can carry disease, especially fungal diseases. These can be deadly on their own, but that's not all. They also lay hundreds of eggs fast, and the larvae will devour plant roots.

Fungus Gnat Prevention
- Inspect plants before you buy them, checking at the base of the plant for signs of the clear or whitish fungus gnat larvae.
- Avoid overwatering your plants.
- Use yellow sticky traps to find adult gnats.
- Mulch your soil to keep adult gnats from laying eggs in the soil.

Organic Fungus Gnat Controls
- Drench the soil with a mixture of water and hydrogen peroxide at a 4:1 ratio.
- Drench soil in a mixture of neem oil and water.
- Use a pyrethrin-based spray to kill fungus gnat larvae.
- Inoculate the soil with beneficial nematodes.

Spider mites are nearly impossible to see until they've built up enough numbers to be a serious problem.

SPIDER MITES

Have you ever had a plant that appears to be starting to turn yellow in patches or has super-fine "webs" all over it, but you can't see any spiders?

If so, you may be at war with a very common pest both indoors and outdoors: spider mites. Spider mites are not a true insect, as is commonly believed; instead, they are a type of arachnid closely related to spiders and ticks. They're extremely tiny; you'll need a magnifying glass to get a good look at them. They cause the undersides of leaves to appear dusty, but if you look closely, you'll see that the dust is actually moving.

Spider Mite Prevention

- Keep your plants watered well so spider mites don't take hold.
- Remove any dust or debris from your plants' leaves at least once a week.
- Keep humidity low and airflow high.

Organic Spider Mite Controls

- Spray your plants with neem oil to smother the mites.
- Use a specific mite control product such as Mite-X.
- Blow concentrated air on your plants with a product like The Bug Blaster.
- Introduce beneficial insects such as predatory mites, ladybugs, or lacewings.

This cotton mealybug looks like something out of a science fiction novel.

If left unchecked, grasshoppers can chomp away entire plants in short order.

SCALE INSECTS AND MEALYBUGS

Eew, scale insects. Whether flat against leaves or fruit, or lumpy bumps on branches or stems, this widespread superfamily of insects is well over 8,000 species strong. Many of them are agricultural pests while others prey on trees or other plant life. What most people don't realize is that mealybugs are a form of scale. Unlike most scale, however, they have legs, but they seldom if ever move once they've located a good feeding spot. Mealybugs are a common greenhouse scale pest.

Scale Insect and Mealybug Prevention

- If you spot a few scale insects, dab them with a cotton swab soaked in rubbing alcohol.
- Prune any infested branches and destroy the branches.

Organic Scale Insect and Mealybug Controls

- Scale insects are resistant to some pesticides, but they will die if they're smothered with horticultural oil.
- Neem oil will both smother and poison scale insects.
- Upgrade to a stronger neem-based product like AzaMax if your scale infestation is severe.
- You can often rub scale insects off your plants if you give them a wash.

GRASSHOPPERS

You've cultivated an amazing garden, full of lush greens and veggies, only to have it relentlessly attacked by grasshoppers. Unlike many garden pests that focus on one type of plant, grasshoppers aren't too picky and can obliterate most of the plants you've spent all season growing.

Grasshoppers can decimate your garden. They eat around 50 percent of their weight every single day. No matter where they are in their life cycle, they'll chew away at both the stems and the leaves of garden plants. If left un-checked, this damage can become severe, leaving your entire garden without leaves, unable to grow.

Adults (which are 1 to 2 inches long) are brown to reddish yellow or green in color with prominent jaws, fully developed wings, and short antennae. They have enlarged hind legs and can jump great distances. Immature stages, or nymphs, are similar in appearance to adults, but are smaller and have wing buds instead of wings.

Grasshopper Prevention

- Till your soil in the spring to destroy overwintering eggs.
- Grow under row covers to protect sensitive plants.

Don't let snails and slugs get out of control or they'll decimate your garden.

Organic Grasshopper Controls
- Use EcoBran bait to attract and kill grasshoppers.
- Use a diluted garlic spray over affected areas of the garden.
- Spray hot pepper wax over grasshopper hot spots.

Slugs and Snails

Slugs and snails love damp, shady spots and become most active at night. They'll munch on your low-growing seedlings and leafy greens. However, they can also attack fruits such as tomatoes or strawberries. Nothing is off limits when it comes to these annoying pests.

Slug and Snail Prevention
- Remove any debris, wood, and weeds from growing areas to remove cover for these pests.
- Water in the morning instead of the evening, as slugs and snails are more active at night and like a moist environment.

Organic Slug and Snail Controls
- Handpick after the sun sets, as this is when they're most active.
- Fill shallow bowls with stale beer and bury them in the soil. The beer will attract slugs and snails, and they will drown.
- Use an organic bait (such as Sluggo).

Encouraging birds to visit the garden with a bird bath and bird feeder helps add another pest control layer to your strategy.

Animals

While insects are the more common garden pests you'll deal with, larger animals can make short work of your garden if left to their own devices.

BIRDS

I actually *welcome* birds in my garden. They're an integral part of the natural ecosystem around a garden, picking plants clean of caterpillars and other larvae. However, many gardeners get frustrated when birds peck holes in their ripe tomatoes or steal their berries.

It's a little-known secret that what birds are actually after when they do this is *water*. My best solution for dealing with birds in the garden is to welcome them with open arms and install a simple bird feeder and bird bath. This way, they get all of the food and water they need. If you do this, the only thing you'll see them doing in your garden is hopping around and having some extra snacks on the bugs, which is *exactly* what you want.

If you *really* want to deter birds from your garden (away from fruits, in particular), use strips of flashing (holographic) repeller ribbon. This is particularly effective against starlings. You can also install bird netting on your berry bushes, as birds often like to pick these clean of your precious fruit.

A family of deer are munching on urban rosebushes (which they love).

DEER

Dealing with deer can be exceptionally frustrating. Each herd tends to prefer different plants based on what's available in their area, and it usually happens to be your favorite ones. That being said, there are some plants they typically don't go for:

- fuzzy, hairy, or spiky plants
- plants with heavy fragrances, like most herbs
- poisonous plants
- most grasses

For you as an urban gardener, those suggestions may not be *too* helpful, because you want to grow edibles . . . the same ones that deer love to munch on. Your second option is to install a deer-proof fence. Fencing is an expensive and time-consuming process, but if you're living in an area where deer are a real presence, it can be worth the investment.

Make sure to build a fence that is:
- at *least* 8 feet tall, as deer can jump up to that height
- opaque, if at all possible, as deer won't jump over what they can't see through

If fencing isn't the route you want to take, you have two more options. First, use tried-and-true deer repellents. Most smell pretty nasty as they're made from rotten eggs, blood, garlic, onion, and/or soap. The goal is to convince the deer that your garden simply doesn't taste very good. The key to success with deer repellents is diligent application. Don't slack or they might be back for a tasty treat.

One of my favorite methods for getting rid of deer also happens to be the most elegant: use a motion-activated sprinkler system. Deer scare easily, and a blast of water to the face as they sneak into your garden is sure to do the trick. Make sure you get a sprinkler system that has an infrared sensor because deer often attack under cover of darkness.

A no-kill groundhog trap allows you to capture these pesky garden pests alive. After capture, call animal control, a professional trapper, or an animal shelter for advice about relocation.

GROUNDHOGS AND GOPHERS

Groundhogs are some of the most frustrating rodents to do battle with in your garden. They decimate your vegetation and hide underground, coming up to snack on your plants and then disappear.

However, hope is not all lost. There are a few techniques that work well against these annoying creatures.

- They can be shy; scare them with wind chimes or reflective objects.
- Use hardware cloth on the bottom of raised beds to prevent underground attacks.
- Set groundhog traps and when you catch them, relocate them a few miles away from your home.
- Fence your entire garden in with rabbit fencing at least to 6 inches tall. To ensure they don't burrow under, bury the fencing at least 18 inches deep.

One last thing—in my experience, the ultrasonic groundhog and gopher repellent devices aren't too effective. Save your money and put in some sweat equity; your garden will thank you.

SQUIRRELS

My first encounter with squirrels was seeing one munch on my prized loquats just as they began to ripen one spring. I figured I had a few days before they got plump and juicy. I was right, but squirrels had the same idea. In just two days, they'd eaten about half of the loquats on my tree, leaving me devastated.

Squirrels aren't picky when it comes to food, snacking on fruits, veggies, insects, and even mushrooms. This means that no matter what you're growing, your garden looks like an all-you-can-eat buffet to a squirrel.

Here are a few tactics to try when dealing with a squirrel infestation:

- Keep the ground clear of falling fruit, nuts, and other food squirrels love.
- Install a fence around your garden, buried at least 12 inches deep.
- Sprinkle dog or human hair in a few spots in the garden. Squirrels seem to hate the smell of human hair and will leave your garden alone.
- Dedicate a specific portion of your garden to the squirrels. If you can't beat them, join them.
- Cover your plants with netting or floating row covers to prevent squirrel access.
- Make sure your bird feeders are out of reach of climbing squirrels, as they'll quickly see it as a source of consistent food.

Just hanging out and munching a snack from a neighbor's garden!

Diseases

If I had to choose my least favorite plant problem to deal with, it'd be diseases. They're often harder to identify and troubleshoot than pests. You can look at a pest, figure out what it is, and then deal with it.

With diseases, it's much harder to figure out what disease you're dealing with and get rid of it—but it's not impossible. Let's learn how to identify, prevent, and control plant diseases.

General Disease Prevention Practices

Before I talk about the top ten most common diseases and how to control them, there are some habits you should get into as a gardener that will dramatically decrease the amount of diseases you'll have in the garden.

FOCUS ON SOIL HEALTH

My number one motto in the garden is this: whenever possible, let Mother Nature do the work for you. By cultivating extremely healthy soil, you're creating a complex ecosystem of microorganisms and beneficial insects that help keep diseases at bay.

SPRAY WITH COMPOST OR WORM TEA

If you're struggling with a nasty bout of powdery mildew or just want to boost your plants with some extra micronutrients, spraying your plants with a batch of compost or worm tea will help. The microorganisms in the tea compete with diseases for the same resources, oftentimes outcompeting them and killing them off. On top of that, your plants will thank you for the nutrition.

SANITIZE YOUR TOOLS

This is an often forgotten tip but it's crucial to prevent spreading disease all over your garden. Mixing 90 percent water with 10 percent bleach and dipping your tools in this solution after using them dramatically reduces the chances you'll spread disease from a sick plant to a healthy one.

WORK "STRONG TO WEAK"

On that note, if you know you have plants in the garden that are suffering from diseases, don't work on those plants first. When doing your daily gardening tasks, work from your healthiest plants to your weakest ones. This way you avoid contaminating plants "up the chain."

DON'T SPLASH YOUR SOIL

Many soilborne diseases make their way onto your plants when soil "splashes" up onto branches, stems, and leaves, where they can start attacking and infecting your plants. The solution is simple: don't aggressively water your plants. Either use drip irrigation or gently water at the soil surface with a hose. You can also prune the bottom of your plants to reduce the chance that soil hits those sensitive areas.

Cabbage leaves suffering from disease is an all too common sight for members of the *Brassica* family.

Anthracnose

Anthracnose is a fungal disease that causes water-soaked spots on all parts of your plants. The center of the spots will develop pink gelatinous masses of spores, which reproduce and spread the disease throughout the garden. It thrives in cool, wet weather and can overwinter in garden debris, soil, and seeds.

ANTHRACNOSE PREVENTION

- Maintain the garden so it's free of debris and dead plant material.
- Space your plants and keep them well pruned to allow for good airflow.
- Water in a way that doesn't splash soil onto your plants.
- Keep fruits off of the soil surface.

Dark spots on a mango leaf are indicative of the early stages of anthracnose.

Damping off is the number one disease you'll face when starting seeds.

ORGANIC ANTHRACNOSE CONTROLS

- Neem oil can help prevent this fungal disease from developing on the surfaces of leaves or stems.
- Organic fungicides with *Bacillus subtilis* can kill fungal growth.
- Consider a liquid copper fungicide to decimate anthracnose.

Damping Off

Damping off is a heartbreaking disease for us gardeners because it targets new seedlings that are just getting started. You'll know your seedlings are suffering from damping off when their stems and roots start to rot at or below the soil surface. Your plants will germinate and sprout just fine, but in two to three days they'll become mushy, fall over, and die. There is no cure for plants that already have damping off, so focus on preventing it from happening in the first place.

DAMPING OFF PREVENTION

- Make sure you're starting seeds in a well-draining seedling mix.
- Don't sow seeds too close together as that will crowd plants and reduce air circulation.
- Bottom-water your new seedlings to avoid too much moisture on top of the soil.
- Add extra air circulation by using a fan when growing indoors.
- Consider sterilizing your soil if your seedlings continue to suffer from damping off.

An example of early blight on tomatoes caused by *Alternaria solani*.

A classic example of powdery mildew taking over a cucumber plant.

Early Blight

Are you finding brown, ringlike spots on your cabbage leaves? Perhaps you're discovering blotches of brown on your tomatoes, or even on your apple or orange trees? You may have alternaria leaf spot.

A common fungal disease in many fruit and vegetable gardens, alternaria can appear in ornamentals as well. It's not particularly discriminatory as to its choice of plant. If the fungal spores land there, and it seems like a good habitat, it will try to colonize.

EARLY BLIGHT PREVENTION

- Remove dead plant matter and dispose of it regularly (as this disease can overwinter).
- Rotate your crops so you plant alternaria-resistant plants where you suffered from it the year before.
- Use drip irrigation to water your plants and avoid soil splashing.
- Plant resistant species in the first place.

ORGANIC EARLY BLIGHT CONTROLS

- Apply a liquid copper fungicide every seven to ten days.
- Cover the tops and bottoms of infected plants with a sulfur-based powder to reduce propagation of the fungal spores.
- Smother your leaves with neem oil spray.

Powdery Mildew

There is possibly no more annoying disease to battle in the garden than the dreaded powdery mildew. It's common on many plants and easy to recognize, with its white-gray powdery coating on the leaves of affected plants. Severe infections will cause leaf browning and eventually kill both leaves and fruits.

Powdery mildew loves young leaves and is almost impossible to completely eradicate from the garden, as its spores can overwinter on plant debris.

The most susceptible plants are beans, cucumbers, squash, pumpkins, tomatoes, and zucchini, so keep a watchful eye over these crops.

POWDERY MILDEW PREVENTION

- Plant resistant varieties of the most susceptible crops.
- Plant in a sunny location with good air circulation.
- Prune the under-canopy of your plants to increase air circulation.
- Remove all diseased or dead plant debris throughout the season and especially at the end of the season.

ORGANIC POWDERY MILDEW CONTROLS

- Spray plant foliage with a 40 percent milk, 60 percent water mixture every one to two weeks (*before* infestation).
- Wash your foliage from time to time to disrupt the life cycle of the disease.
- Water in the morning, preferably with drip irrigation or without splashing soil on your plants.
- Burn or throw away any diseased plant debris instead of composting it.
- Use copper- or sulfur-based fungicides for severe infections.

Downy mildew is attacking this cucumber leaf. Notice its different look compared to powdery mildew.

This is an example of a particularly bad case of blossom end rot.

Downy Mildew

Downy mildew and powdery mildew are often confused for the other, but they are completely separate problems in the garden. Downy mildew appears as yellowish/whitish patches on older leaves. On the undersides of these leaves, the fungus shows up as a whitish/grayish cottony mass. Eventually, the disease causes leaves to brown, become crisp, and die.

Downy mildew *loves* cool weather with high humidity. It typically strikes at the shoulders of the season during early spring or late fall.

DOWNY MILDEW PREVENTION

- Keep your plants pruned well to improve air circulation.
- Never water the foliage of susceptible plants.
- Stake your plants well so they don't collapse on themselves and decrease airflow.
- Grow varieties that are resistant to downy mildew.
- Clear any and all plant debris from the soil surface.

ORGANIC DOWNY MILDEW CONTROLS

- Use neem oil as a first line of defense to stop early infections from taking over a plant.
- Use an organic copper fungicide every seven to ten days to control more severe infections.
- Destroy extremely diseased plants.

Blossom End Rot

There's nothing more frustrating than seeing your beautiful heirloom tomatoes suffering from a nasty black spot at the bottom of the fruit. Blossom end rot is not so much a disease as it is a symptom of a problem with your plant's growing environment. It affects peppers, cucumbers, and eggplants too.

You'll notice the bottoms of these fruits starting to turn mushy, eventually becoming brown or black, with a leathery texture. It's brought about by a calcium deficiency. However, the solution isn't necessarily amending your soil with calcium. Uneven watering practices can create a calcium transport issue in plants, which leads to blossom end rot.

BLOSSOM END ROT PREVENTION

Because blossom end rot isn't a disease, it can't be treated. Your best bet is to prevent it from occurring in the first place by following these best practices:

- Keep your soil evenly moist at all times to avoid calcium transport issues.
- Foliar spray your plants with a liquid kelp or compost tea.
- Add extra calcium to your soil when you plant seeds or seedlings (bone meal, egg shells, or gypsum are good options).
- Add mulch to prevent moisture loss from the soil.
- Avoid overfertilizing plants with heavy amounts of nitrogen, as this can interfere with calcium uptake.

Appendix

Urban Gardening Mistakes to Avoid

All gardeners, new and old, will run into some classic mistakes from time to time. Gardening is both a simple and a complicated hobby at the same time, so, naturally, mistakes will happen. I've killed more plants than I care to admit to you, but every time I make a mistake, I try to understand why it happened and file it away in my mental drawer of gardening knowledge.

Let's go over some common mistakes and missteps that you might make in the garden.

Watering Problems

Without a doubt, watering is the most troubling and error-prone part of the gardening process. There are so many ways to mess it up, all of which are easy to avoid if you follow these simple rules.

KEEP YOUR SOIL EVENLY MOIST

Some plants you'll grow prefer even moisture levels and will start to stress if the soil gets bone dry, then floods, and the cycle repeats. One of the best ways to ensure even moisture is to use an organic mulch such as straw, grass clippings, or wood chips. Not only is mulch a great way to prevent water loss via evaporation, but organic mulches eventually break down into organic matter and work their way into your soil, improving it over time.

WATER LESS OFTEN, BUT DEEPER

Many gardeners think that watering every day is the way to go. That couldn't be further from the truth. If you water *deeply* and employ good water conservation techniques such as mulching, you can get away with watering much less often. Water that reaches the subsoil doesn't evaporate as quickly and is also in the perfect location to be used by a plant's root system.

WATER IN THE MORNING > EVENING > AFTERNOON

If you're a morning person—unlike me—you'll be happy to learn that the early morning is, hands down, the best time to water a vegetable garden (or any other garden, for that matter).

The reason is simple; in the morning, the sun is barely up and temperatures are still cool. Water has time to actually penetrate the soil and reach the root systems of your garden without being lost to evaporation.

Watering early also protects your plants from intense heat in the middle of the day, as they will be full of water by the time the heat actually hits them. This is much better than trying to "save" your plants on a hot day by pouring water on them in the afternoon.

If, like me, you're not much of a morning person, then water in the late afternoon or early evening. The principle here is clear: you're trying to do whatever you can to avoid watering in the middle of the day.

While watering at the end of the day is slightly worse than the morning, if you have no other option it's certainly better than not watering at all.

If you decide to water in the evening, do your best not to get water all over your plants' leaves. Damp leaves is the cause of the spread of many pathogens and diseases, such as the dreaded powdery mildew that can decimate an entire garden.

If you can avoid it, don't water at night. The biggest reason why is what I previously mentioned—you are dampening leaves and plant matter at night, when little to no evaporation will occur. This is a great recipe for diseases and rot, but it's not a good recipe for a healthy garden.

If you absolutely can't wait, then sure . . . water at night. But use a bit less water than you normally would because there will be no evaporation. That means all of the water you pour onto the soil will sink in and be used by your plants.

WATER, WAIT, AND WATER AGAIN

One classic mistake new gardeners make is dumping a ton of water onto their garden in a few seconds and considering the job done. This couldn't be further from the truth.

Soil needs a second to absorb the initial burst of water. Watering quickly will lead to a lot of runoff, which wastes water and keeps your plants thirsty for more.

To avoid this, water lightly to wet the soil surface, wait a minute or two—and then water more. Your soil will soak up *far* more water this way, and your plants will thank you for it.

AUTOMATE YOUR WATERING

The best way to water is not to water at all—at least, not by hand. Drip irrigation in combination with timers is one of the best ways to put the chore of watering out of your mind.

Planting Mistakes

Aside from watering, there are a few simple errors you might make out of inexperience or lack of planning that make gardening more of a headache. Planting mistakes are important to watch out for, because mistakes made in this phase of your gardening journey will compound and can potentially ruin an entire growing season.

NOT LABELING YOUR PLANTS

This might seem like a no-brainer, but you'd be surprised how often you can forget to label what you're planting and where you're planting it. I like to label my seedlings with plant stakes both in my trays and in the ground after I transplant.

Follow this up with making notes in a garden journal, and you'll never forget where and when you planted your veggies.

GROWING PLANTS YOU DON'T LIKE TO EAT

This is another tip that seems obvious but is ignored all of the time. When I first started gardening, I grew plants I thought you "should" grow as a gardener, completely ignoring the fact that I wasn't a big fan of them when it came time to harvest. Pick plants that you already use in your cooking or know you like. That way, you'll actually care about growing them well and will enjoy the harvest.

NOT READING THE SEED PACKET

Seed packets are easy to ignore but they are packed with information that can be confusing at first glance. Be sure to give them a thorough read, though. Every plant requires slightly different care, spacing, and planting depth; you'll never know unless you look.

GROWING PLANTS OUT OF SEASON

This is a mistake I've made a million times, eager to squeeze one last batch of tomatoes from the garden as fall approaches. Whether you go to your local nursery or buy seeds, it's easy to be tempted to plant out of season, "Just to see what happens."

Don't do it. You'll end up putting a lot of effort into a plant that you may never get to harvest. If you plant spinach in the middle of the summer, it will bolt quickly and turn bitter before you can harvest a single leaf. Similarly, growing heat-loving okra as you enter the fall is a recipe for disaster and frustration.

Maintenance Mistakes

As the saying goes, "An ounce of prevention is worth a pound of cure." However, in gardening, if you don't put in the ounce of prevention, you may not even have the opportunity for a pound of cure. As a general rule, I recommend spending ten to twenty minutes a day in the garden, inspecting your plants, checking the soil, and keeping a watchful eye open for pests and diseases. It's a great way to bookend the day, spending a bit of time in the morning and evening caring for your plant babies.

NOT HARVESTING YOUR PLANTS

This might seem like a crazy mistake to make, but believe me, I've seen it happen countless times. As a beginner urban gardener, don't be hesitant to actually harvest what you grow. When you're growing heavy producers, such as beans or peas, be sure to harvest early and often to spur more harvests as the weeks go by.

(continued)

(continued)

GIVING WEEDS A FREE PASS

It's tempting to let your eyes glance over the odd weed here and there, but believe me when I say this is a major mistake. If left unchecked, weeds can establish themselves to a degree that you can't imagine . . . until you experience it. When you're out in the garden doing your daily maintenance, pluck any and all weeds you see the instant they pop up.

NOT DESTROYING DISEASED PLANTS

I know, I know . . . it *physically* hurts to get rid of a plant that's come under the weather. However, most diseases can and will spread easily to other plants in the garden. Pretty soon, what was one squash plant with powdery mildew has become an entire bed covered in the white, dusty disease. As soon as a plant crosses the point of no return disease-wise, it's time to destroy it. Pull it out and throw it in the trash or the fire pit . . . it's not worth the risk.

Here are some of the tried-and-true companies, products, and brands that I love. Feel free to tell them Kevin from Epic Gardening sent you!

Trusted Brands
- Gardener's Supply Company: www.gardeners.com
- Johnny's Selected Seeds: www.johnnyseeds.com
- Bootstrap Farmer: www.bootstrapfarmer.com

My Favorite Seed Companies
- Baker Creek Heirloom Seeds: www.rareseeds.com
- San Diego Seed Company: www.sandiegoseedcompany.com
- Urban Farmer Seeds: www.ufseeds.com

Raised Beds
- Birdies Garden Products: www.birdiesgardenproducts.com

Organic Fertilizers
- Garden Maker Naturals: www.gardenmaker.com
- Old Truck Organics: www.oldtruckorganics.com

Microgreen Seed Suppliers
- True Leaf Market: www.trueleafmarket.com
- Everwilde Farms: www.everwilde.com

Vermicomposting
- Urban Worm Company: www.urbanwormcompany.com
- SproutFaster: www.sproutfaster.com

Hydroponics
- Aponix Vertical Barrel: www.aponix.eu
- HydroFarm: www.hydrofarm.com
- General Hydroponics: www.generalhydroponics.com

Grow Lights
- Soltech Solutions: www.soltechsolutionsllc.com
- The Green Sunshine Company: www.thegreensunshineco.com

Metric Conversions

Metric Equivalent

Inches (in.)	1/64	1/32	1/25	1/16	1/8	1/4	3/8	2/5	1/2	5/8	3/4	7/8	1	2	3	4	5	6	7	8	9	10	11	12	36	39.4
Feet (ft.)																								1	3	3 1/12
Yards (yd.)																									1	1 1/12
Millimeters (mm)	0.40	0.79	1	1.59	3.18	6.35	9.53	10	12.7	15.9	19.1	22.2	25.4	50.8	76.2	101.6	127	152	178	203	229	254	279	305	914	1,000
Centimeters (cm)							0.95	1	1.27	1.59	1.91	2.22	2.54	5.08	7.62	10.16	12.7	15.2	17.8	20.3	22.9	25.4	27.9	30.5	91.4	100
Meters (m)																								.30	.91	1.00

Converting Measurements

TO CONVERT:	TO:	MULTIPLY BY:
Inches	Millimeters	25.4
Inches	Centimeters	2.54
Feet	Meters	0.305
Yards	Meters	0.914
Miles	Kilometers	1.609
Square inches	Square centimeters	6.45
Square feet	Square meters	0.093
Square yards	Square meters	0.836
Cubic inches	Cubic centimeters	16.4
Cubic feet	Cubic meters	0.0283
Cubic yards	Cubic meters	0.765
Pints (U.S.)	Liters	0.473 (Imp. 0.568)
Quarts (U.S.)	Liters	0.946 (Imp. 1.136)
Gallons (U.S.)	Liters	3.785 (Imp. 4.546)
Ounces	Grams	28.4
Pounds	Kilograms	0.454
Tons	Metric tons	0.907

TO CONVERT:	TO:	MULTIPLY BY:
Millimeters	Inches	0.039
Centimeters	Inches	0.394
Meters	Feet	3.28
Meters	Yards	1.09
Kilometers	Miles	0.621
Square centimeters	Square inches	0.155
Square meters	Square feet	10.8
Square meters	Square yards	1.2
Cubic centimeters	Cubic inches	0.061
Cubic meters	Cubic feet	35.3
Cubic meters	Cubic yards	1.31
Liters	Pints (U.S.)	2.114 (Imp. 1.76)
Liters	Quarts (U.S.)	1.057 (Imp. 0.88)
Liters	Gallons (U.S.)	0.264 (Imp. 0.22)
Grams	Ounces	0.035
Kilograms	Pounds	2.2
Metric tons	Tons	1.1

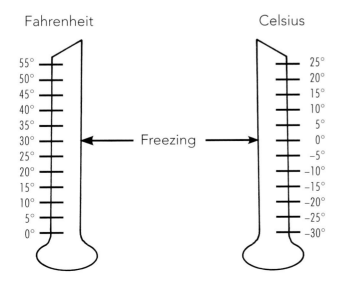

Fahrenheit — Celsius — Freezing

Converting Temperatures

Convert degrees Fahrenheit (F) to degrees Celsius (C) by following this simple formula: Subtract 32 from the Fahrenheit temperature reading. Then multiply that number by $5/9$. For example, 77°F - 32 = 45. 45 × $5/9$ = 25°C.

To convert degrees Celsius to degrees Fahrenheit, multiply the Celsius temperature reading by $9/5$, then add 32. For example, 25°C × $9/5$ = 45. 45 + 32 = 77°F.

Acknowledgments

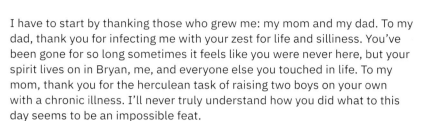

I have to start by thanking those who grew me: my mom and my dad. To my dad, thank you for infecting me with your zest for life and silliness. You've been gone for so long sometimes it feels like you were never here, but your spirit lives on in Bryan, me, and everyone else you touched in life. To my mom, thank you for the herculean task of raising two boys on your own with a chronic illness. I'll never truly understand how you did what to this day seems to be an impossible feat.

To Bryan, my brother. Thank you for being the impetus behind my journey into gardening. I didn't know it at the time, but that summer growing plants with you set me on a path that changed my life forever.

To Jon, my cousin. Thank you for being a "second brain" off of which I can relentlessly bounce all of my crazy ideas and theories.

To my grandma. Thank you for being an example of how to live a truly joyous, fulfilled, and happy life, no matter what gets thrown at you.

To my cousins Elyssa, Lauren, Jaclyn, Taylor, Jordan, Chelsea, Jordan, Julia, and Matt. Thanks for being such great influences throughout my life and for always inspiring me to live a life at "the top."

To Mel Bartholomew. You may be gone, but your gardening spirit lives on in me and in the millions of people you inspired to grow a greener world. Thank you for taking a chance on a young and eager kid.

To Shawna Coronado. Thank you for taking me under your wing and connecting me to The Quarto Group. In the most literal way, this book would not exist without you. I owe you more than a few cocktails!

To Mark, Meredith, Regina, and the rest of the Quarto team. Thank you for your hard work in bringing this book to life, as well as walking a total outsider through the world of traditional publishing.

To Tucker and Zach. Thank you for the opportunity to work with you at Scribe. Without those eighteen months of hard work, observation, and personal growth, Epic Gardening wouldn't be anywhere close to what it is today.

To the Triumvirate: Thank you for being the best support system a guy could ask for.

And finally, to the Epic Gardening community. It is because of each and every one of you that I get to be a crazy plant man for a living. Thank you for all of your emails, comments, messages, letters, phone calls, and connections. I'm so grateful to be connected to so many of you on a personal level and will do my best to keep helping you grow epic plants as the years roll on.

About the Author

Ever since that fateful day that I decided to grow cucumbers and basil with my brother, gardening has been an integral part of my life. Once I connected the simple love of growing plants—be they edible or ornamental—to the larger-scale implications of that action, my life changed forever.

The ability to grow your own food in the comfort of your own home, *no matter where you live*, is a superpower. It's a small act that, when done by millions of people around the world, has an incredible effect upon the way our society moves forward.

In my own life, my front-yard garden has become a neighborhood talking point, starting conversations with passersby that would have never been started otherwise. It's helped cultivate not only delicious and nutritious food for myself, my friends, and my family but also *true community* in a society where that seems to be a lost art.

I've become more connected to my own health, learning how to prepare garden-fresh recipes with produce harvested just minutes before bringing it into the kitchen. I waste less food because I understand on an intimate level the effort that goes into producing it.

I feel a connection to nature that's hard to come by in an urban environment. Bees buzz, birds chirp and pick at pesky caterpillars, and beneficial insects float by as I do my morning walk through the garden.

If you'd like to continue on your urban gardening journey, I highly encourage you to check out the following:

- **The Epic Gardening website. On my site, you'll find hundreds of in-depth articles on growing specific plants, preventing pests and diseases, and many other gardening tips. www.epicgardening.com**
- **The *Epic Gardening* podcast. Each daily five- to ten-minute episode focuses on a specific gardening tip. www.epicgardening.com/podcast**
- **The *Epic Gardening* YouTube channel. In-depth videos show how to grow plants from seed to harvest as well as other gardening topics. www.youtube.com/c/epicgardening**

I hope with all of my heart that this book has given you the tools you need to build beautiful gardens that produce tons of delicious, nutritious food, no matter where you live.

Keep Growing,
Kevin Espiritu

Index